CW00506329

A
Cellarful
of
Noise

A Cellarful of Noise

Brian Epstein

SOUVENIR
PRESS

This edition first published in 2021 by
Souvenir Press,
an imprint of PROFILE BOOKS LTD
29 Cloth Fair
London
EC1A 7JQ
www.souvenirpress.co.uk

First published in Great Britain in 1964 by Souvenir Press

Copyright © Brian Epstein, 1964
Introduction copyright © Craig Brown, 2021

10 9 8 7 6 5 4 3 2 1

Typeset in 11.75/14.5pt Freight Text by MacGuru Ltd
Designed by Barneby Ltd
Printed and bound in Great Britain by Clays Ltd, Elcograf S.p.A.

The moral right of the author has been asserted.

All rights reserved. Without limiting the rights under copyright
reserved above, no part of this publication may be reproduced,
stored or introduced into a retrieval system, or transmitted, in any
form or by any means (electronic, mechanical, photocopying,
recording or otherwise), without the prior written permission of
both the copyright owner and the publisher of this book.

A CIP record for this book can be obtained from the British Library

ISBN: 978 1 80081 118 8
eISBN: 978 1 80081 211 6

FSC
www.fsc.org
MIX
Paper from
responsible sources
FSC® C018072

Contents

Introduction

With his polite side-parting, unflashy suits, diffident manner and public-school accent, Brian Epstein appeared much more mature than the Beatles. In interviews, he would call them 'my boys' or 'the boys'; they, in turn, would always refer to him as 'Mr Epstein'.

So it comes as a surprise to realise he was only six years older than John and Ringo. In April 1964, when he embarked on this memoir, he was twenty-nine. That same month, the top five places in the American top ten were all occupied by the Beatles, and there were a further seven Beatles' singles in the top one hundred, along with two songs about them – 'We Love You Beatles' by the Carefrees and 'A Letter to the Beatles' by the Four Preps.

Since February, they had become the four most famous young men in the world. Even Ringo Starr, the least prepossessing of the Beatles, had been made the subject of a song, 'Ringo, I Love You', written and produced by Phil Spector and sung by Bobbie Jo Mason, soon to become more famous as Cher.

Having engineered all this fame, Epstein was clearly in no mood to play it down. In *A Cellarful of Noise* he describes the Beatles as 'a worldwide phenomenon, like nothing in any of our lifetimes, and like nothing any of us will ever see again'. Mixing condescension with a dash of hyperbole he writes, 'The haunted, wonderful wistful eyes of little Ringo Starr from Liverpool's Dingle are more instantly recognisable than any single feature of any of the world's great statesmen.'

A Cellarful of Noise is a period piece. At times the period seems much earlier than the 1960s, exhibiting the muscular snobbery of John Buchan or Baden-Powell. At one point Epstein declares that the Beatles 'never sit while a woman stands' and at another that 'their naturalness ... wins them the admiration of people like Lord Montgomery'. Of one of his artistes, Gerry Marsden, he boasts that 'Princess Alexandra twice requested him for cabaret at society balls'. Many of his observations about the world of pop are now as dated as the National Milk Bar in Liverpool where he and the boys tucked into four packets of biscuits to celebrate the promise of a recording session at EMI. 'The disc charts cannot stand very many girls,' he writes, 'however gorgeous they may look on stage.'

Nearly sixty years on, the Beatles are still part of the air we breathe, but some of Epstein's other artistes, as he always called them, have vanished without trace. Who remembers Tommy Quickly? Epstein confidently predicts 'he is going to be a star', but alas he never was. Taken up by Epstein, he left his job as a telephone fitter, changed his name from Quigley to Quickly, took part in three Beatles tours and recorded five singles, all flops. He retired from the music business in 1965.

Michael Haslam – 'he, I believe, is going to be very big' – was part of the Beatles Christmas Show at the Hammersmith Odeon for three weeks in 1963. He recorded two unsuccessful singles, both produced by George Martin, the last of which was called, ominously, 'There Goes the Forgotten Man'. Eventually, he fell out with Brian Epstein over an expenses claim for a pair of socks. Epstein let him go, and in 1966 Haslam returned to his £15-a-week job on a fleshing machine at Walker and Martin's tannery in Weston Street, Bolton. His fellow workers greeted his return with a jaunty banner that read, 'Welcome back Mike. Top of the Flops.'

In contrast to the devil-may-care merriment of the Beatles, Brian Epstein cultivated a reserved, fastidious air. He wore a Burberry raincoat, well-polished buckled shoes, gold cufflinks, a monogrammed shirt and a Christian Dior silk tie or a polka-dot cravat. 'He was immaculate from head to toe, like Cary Grant,' recalled Cilla Black. 'He was everything you wanted a posh fella to look like.' His Liverpool tailor, George Hayes, maintained that he always looked as if he'd just stepped out of the bath.

Epstein would have preferred Godfrey Winn or Beverley Nichols, well-manicured household names, to ghost-write his memoir, but his publisher, Ernest Hecht, vetoed them for being 'far too pricey and the wrong image'. In the end, Epstein settled for Derek Taylor, then a showbiz journalist on the *Daily Express* but soon to become the Beatles' press officer.

The two men motored down to the Imperial Hotel, Torquay in Epstein's chauffeur-driven Rolls-Royce. Taylor was particularly impressed by the electric windows. 'I'd never seen such a thing.' The two men got on well. In their first session Epstein opened up about his uneasy childhood and troubled adolescence, but he hesitated before revealing his greatest secret. There came a point when he realised he would have to broach the subject. Over lunch, he suddenly asked, 'Did you know that I was queer?' 'No, I didn't,' replied Taylor. 'Well, I am, and if we're going to do this book I'm going to have to stop buggering about saying I was with this girl when I would not be with a girl, it would be a boy. Does that make any difference?'

It must have been an agonising confession – in 1964 homosexuality was still an imprisonable offence – but Taylor was unfazed. 'No,' he remembered saying, 'it doesn't make any difference. It'll make it a lot easier. So you mustn't worry any more, difficult as it may be to convince you perhaps, but I won't ever let you down.'

Between the two of them, they conspired to render everything seemly. The book makes no mention of Epstein's sexuality or the deep torment it caused him. Of his time in National Service, for instance, we hear simply that he was 'the lousiest soldier in the world'. Wearing a pinstriped suit and a bowler hat, he was charged with impersonating an officer and confined to barracks. This caused his nerves to become 'seriously upset'. Psychiatrists decided he was 'a compulsive civilian and quite unfit for military service', so he was 'discharged on medical grounds'.

The truth is both more fraught and more interesting. Stationed at the Albany Barracks in Regent's Park, Epstein had hated his 'hideous' private's uniform and had asked his tailor to run him up a rather more elegant officer's outfit, which he then wore to cruise the West End in search of young men. At the Army and Navy Club on Piccadilly, military police arrested him and charged him with impersonating an officer. His parents employed lawyers, who succeeded in saving him from a court martial. He was eventually discharged for being 'emotionally and mentally unfit' – code for homosexuality.

Elsewhere in the book Epstein claims, 'I lost a girlfriend called Rita Harris who worked for me and who said, "I'm not going to compete with four kids who think they're entering the big time".' In reality, 'Rita' was a boy.

In his unpublished diaries he was much less guarded, confessing that, after leaving the army, 'My life became a succession of mental illnesses and sordid, unhappy events bringing great sorrow to my family.' It now seems probable that his sexuality led to his torment and his torment led, eventually, to his death. John Lennon's school friend Pete Shotton noted, 'Not only was Brian homosexual; he was sexually aroused by precisely those traits that otherwise most affronted or menaced him: qualities like vulgarity, insolence, callousness, and aggressiveness, all so abundantly on display in the persona of the Beatles' rhythm guitarist ... Brian Epstein was irredeemably mesmerised by the one whose demeanour most resembled that of a caged animal.'

True to character, John Lennon taunted him about the memoir. When Epstein was wondering out loud what to call it, Lennon said, 'Why don't you call it *Queer Jew*?' Later, when Epstein said it was called *A Cellarful of Noise*, Lennon replied that he would be better off calling it *A Cellarful of Boys*.

The self-portrait in *A Cellarful of Noise* may be partial, but it is not untrue. Epstein portrays himself as lonely, businesslike, scrupulous, obsessive, shrewd, awkward and pernickety, all of which he was. Now that we know how his story ended, the odd phrase flashes on the page like a fork of lightning. Quite late in the book, he confesses that the strain of being in sole charge of management 'continues and increases and thrives like a malignant disease'. Soon after, he talks of the pressures he is under. 'The chief of them is loneliness, for ultimately I must bear the strain alone, not only in the office or the theatre, but at home in the small hours.'

He was fanatical, in both senses of the word. When he writes 'I can think of no warmer experience than to be in a vast audience at a Beatles concert' he is guilty only of understatement. The four Beatles were everything he could never be. He told an interviewer in 1964 that the Beatles 'represented the direct, unselfconscious, good-natured, uninhibited human relationships which I hadn't found and had wanted and felt deprived of. And my own sense of inferiority evaporated with the Beatles because I knew I could help them, and that they wanted me to help them, and trusted me to help them.'

Simon Napier-Bell, manager of the Yardbirds, Wham! and many others, once recalled Epstein telling him that at a Beatles stadium concert in America 'he went into the crowd of girls and he just screamed like one of the girls, which he said is what he'd always wanted to do from the first minute he'd ever seen them. He had spent his whole life being restrained and wearing suits and suddenly he just screamed and became the mad fan he wanted to be.'

John, Paul, George and Ringo sometimes went wild, and sometimes behaved foolishly, but they were always able to adapt and move on. They were survivors. Each of them was equipped with a safety valve. But for all his extraordinary abilities, for all his carefully buttoned-up exterior, Brian Epstein was not. He could manage others, but he could never manage himself; he lived in perpetual jeopardy. He took drugs – uppers, downers, acid, heroin, coke – far more recklessly than his boys, and was known to gamble away £20,000 in a single night. Nor could he resist picking up the type of young man who would steal from him, beat him up and blackmail him.

'Eppy seems to be in a terrible state,' John told Pete Shotton one night. 'The guy's head's a total mess, and we're all really worried about him.' John then played a tape. Pete described it as 'one of the most harrowing performances I've ever heard', adding,

The recording was barely recognisable as that of a human voice, alternately groaning, grunting and shrieking words which, even when decipherable, made no apparent sense whatsoever. The man on the tape was obviously suffering from great emotional stress, and very likely under the influence of some extremely potent drugs.

'What the fuck's all that, John?' I said incredulously.

'Don't you recognise the voice? That's Brian. He made the tape for me in his house. I don't know why he sent it, but he's trying to tell me something – fuck knows what. He just can't seem to communicate with us in his usual way any more.'

Three years after the publication of *A Cellarful of Noise*, on Sunday 27 August 1967, Brian Epstein was found dead in the bedroom of his house in Belgravia. Two brief suicide notes were found, hidden away in a book, but they were both dated several weeks before. At the inquest his psychiatrist Dr Flood reported that 'his main complaint was insomnia, anxiety and depression'. Epstein had, he said, 'always shown some signs of emotional instability ... The patient was homosexual, but had been unable to come to terms with this problem.' Recording a verdict of accidental death, the coroner said that it was due to poisoning by the sedative Carbitral, caused by an incautious self-overdose.

Together, the Beatles went round to comfort Brian's mother, Queenie. They wanted to attend his funeral, but Queenie dreaded it turning into a media circus, and thought it best if they stayed away. 'They were like four lost children,' she recalled.

In the vast Beatles Story Museum in Liverpool, just

around the corner from the cabinet containing the four *Sgt. Pepper* costumes and housed in a glass case of its own, stands a dapper knee-length blue coat with three shiny buttons. It dresses a headless mannequin. A little triangle of sharp white shirt and a paisley tie poke out through the top. The caption on the cabinet reads, 'Brian's wool and cashmere coat made by Aquascutum of Regent Street'.

Had he lived, Brian Epstein would now be pushing ninety. He would probably control the Beatles Story Museum and have ensured the Beatles a decent share of the profits. He would undoubtedly have expanded his empire. Over the past fifty-odd years society's misgivings about his homosexuality would have transformed into qualifications. By now he would be Sir Brian Epstein, or perhaps even Lord Epstein of Belgravia, a valued board member of the Garrick Club, Tate Modern and the Liverpool Institute of Performing Arts.

Instead, he lies buried in Everton Cemetery, while his Aquascutum coat, spick and span as ever, retains a life of its own, resplendent under a spotlight in its glass case, admired by 300,000 people a year. It is a modern relic or, in sacramental terms, an outward sign of inward grace. In gold letters, embossed on the bottom of the case, is a quote from Paul McCartney: 'If anyone was the fifth Beatle, it was Brian.'

—Craig Brown

Author's Note

Reading through my proofs it occurs to me that I'm going to be asked why in the midst of a busy life I should take time off from the personal management of my artistes, to whom, after all, I have signed myself, to write my own autobiography when I'm not yet thirty. Like every pointed query of that nature, the answer can be manifold. But principally it is simply that I wanted to put down at an early stage an accurate account of the emergence of the Beatles and others from my own point of view. So much has been said that is exaggerated, inaccurate, extravagant and open to misinterpretation that I thought that a detailed account could only help and, I hope, prove of considerable public interest. Anyway I enjoyed doing it and I sometimes think that the essence of a creation, be it a book, a disc or a live stage performance, is just that.

Last night I returned from a hectic 72-hour trip to New York. I went to tie up final details of the Beatles' US tour and to arrange another jointly by Gerry and the Pacemakers and Billy J. Kramer with his Dakotas in the fall. Also to see about what may prove to be the most exciting American venture ... Cilla in cabaret in Washington and New York.

It's not impossible that having smugly written an account of the advent of so many successful discs, my luck may change. If it does, it does, and I shall devote my endeavour to ensuring the continuance of my artistes as major entertainers as long as they may wish me to do so.

And I'd like to put on record that I'm very much aware that this book could not possibly have been written without some people who I most sincerely and gratefully acknowledge:

My Mother, Father and Brother
All the artistes I manage
The young people of Merseyside

And last but very much not least Derek Taylor, for whose invaluable help with the preparation of this book and his professional experience I am greatly indebted.

Belgravia, London, August, 1964

Prologue

At about three o'clock on Saturday, 28 October 1961, an eighteen-year-old boy called Raymond Jones, wearing jeans and black leather jacket, walked into a record store in Whitechapel, Liverpool, and said: 'There's a record I want. It's "My Bonnie" and it was made in Germany. Have you got it?'

Behind the counter was Brian Epstein, twenty-seven, director of the store. He shook his head. 'Who is the record by?' he asked. 'You won't have heard of them,' said Jones. 'It's by a group called the Beatles ...'

1

Beatles – USA

The group of young musicians who could neither read music nor write it, and who are known as the Beatles, conquered the United States of America on 7 February 1964, and by implication – since America is the heart and soul of popular music – the Beatles ruled the pop world.

By May this year the Beatles had become a worldwide phenomenon, like nothing in any of our lifetimes, and like nothing any of us will ever see again. If there was a turning point in their career – a specific date on which the breadth and scope of their future was to be altered – then it was the day their Pan-American Clipper touched down at John F. Kennedy Airport, in New York, to a welcome which has seldom been equalled anywhere in history.

Nobody – certainly not me, though my optimism was persistent from the very start – could have foreseen the excitement and the drama, and the incredible curiosity aroused by the arrival on American soil of these four long-haired lads from Liverpool.

I remember very well the night earlier that month in Paris, when a cable arrived from New York which said simply, 'Beatles Number one in Cashbox Record Chart, New York with "I Want to Hold Your Hand".' We simply could not believe it. For years the Beatles, like every other British artiste, had watched the American charts with remote envy. The American charts were the unobtainable. Only Stateside artistes ever made any imprint. And yet I had known that if the Beatles were to mean anything in America, and if the Beatles were to make a record which would sell in America, then 'I Want to Hold Your Hand' was that record.

At all stages of the Beatles' career, I and they seemed to have reached what we believed to be the ultimate – first of all it was the recording contract with EMI, way back in 1962. This, to us, was the greatest thing that could happen. Then it was the success of their first record; but this of course was only the beginning. The next ultimate was the number-one position of 'Please Please Me'. There could be, we believed then, nothing more important or dramatic or thrilling than to be number one in the British record charts. But one goes on and on and – with the qualities of the Beatles – upwards and upwards, and our next high spot was the first appearance on *Sunday Night at the London Palladium* – the top television show in Europe.

So what's left? Came November 1963 and the Beatles were selected for the *Royal Variety Show* before the Queen Mother. Another ultimate ...

With all this behind us so few things seem to remain for them to conquer. Always America seemed too big, too vast, too remote and too American. I remember the night we heard about the number-one position in Cashbox, I said to John Lennon, 'There can be nothing more important than this,' adding a tentative, 'Can there?'

A journalist sitting nearby, eavesdropping as journalists do, said, 'Well, Carnegie Hall would be fairly big.' And even then, though we knew we were on the way to some sort of eminence in America, we rejected this because Carnegie Hall was surely the world's greatest concert platform, rarely, so far as we knew, accessible to pop artistes, however great.

But on Wednesday, 12 February, the Beatles topped the bill at this great hall, and a few days earlier I had been forced by pressure of commitments to turn down an offer of several thousand pounds for the Beatles to appear at Madison Square Gardens in New York! We were living in a state of extreme turbulence and excitement which left everybody, except the bland, down-to-earth Beatles, reeling and dazed.

Operation USA started in November 1963, so far as I was concerned. The Beatles have always been happy to leave timings, plots, plans, schemes and the development of their career to me because they were good enough to trust me and because they knew that if there was some important decision to make I would consult them to sound their remarkable instincts and to gauge their reactions.

In November, I took Billy J. Kramer – another very successful British artiste whom I had signed in Liverpool – to New York, first of all to promote him and secondly – and more importantly as it turned out – to find out why the Beatles, who were the biggest thing the British pop world had ever known, hadn't 'happened' in America.

As I said, I did not imagine that they would be the immediate answer to Sinatra, but I did think they would have made some little mark on show business over there because their charm and their musical ability were undeniable, and in America there has always been a receptivity to talent.

The trip for Billy J. Kramer cost me £2,000 because I booked into an extremely good hotel and we lived demonstratively and well in order to impress the Americans that we were people of some importance. Actually, of course, we were people of no great importance to the Americans. We were two ordinary travellers – nobody knew me and I didn't know anybody over there beyond three contacts whose names were in my pocketbook.

It was like London in the early days and, as in London in 1962, I started the rounds of the various companies – the television people, the recording firms – and the first people I spoke to were Vee-Jay. During this time, of course, the Beatles were becoming very big in England.

The press had started to write about what they termed Beatlemania in October as a result of the Palladium and the *Royal Show*, and little news items were beginning to filter through to New York and into the American press, and I learned that it was pretty well decided that the next Beatles record – previously they had had no success on the two labels for whom they had recorded – was going to be issued on Capitol.

I went to Vee-Jay, however, because they had done a

very good job for Frank Ifield who was a successful young British star. But of course Ifield had only limited success in America, like every other British artiste since the war. There had always been some curious deficiency in British pop stars as far as the Americans were concerned. The view was that whatever the British did at their best, an American at his best would do very much better.

Moving around New York I found that there was without question an American 'sound' on disc which appealed to the American public. If you have an instinct for this sort of thing – and I believe, modestly, that I have – you can sense these things. I believe I know a British hit and in November I felt that there was a certain American *feeling*. This feeling, I was certain, existed in 'I Want to Hold Your Hand'.

Recording is the core of pop music and I felt very strongly that 'I Want to Hold Your Hand' was going to be a success – however moderate – in the USA.

But I still persisted with other companies because one had learned not to rely on one outlet. I contacted Walter Hofer who has since become my American attorney, and, more important than anything else so far as the Beatles' visual impact was concerned, I met Ed Sullivan.

This came about because there was an enquiry from the Talent Officers' Room at CBS almost on my arrival in New York. I made an arrangement to see Sullivan and on the same day had a call from a leading British agent asking me if I would like him to fix an *Ed Sullivan Show* for the Beatles. I turned this down because I preferred to do direct business and this policy paid off.

I went to see Ed Sullivan at his hotel in New York and I found him a most genial fellow. After a lot of discussion we arranged bookings for three *Ed Sullivan Shows* for the Beatles and two *Ed Sullivan Shows* for Gerry and the Pacemakers, and a fine working and personal relationship was set up between the two of us.

There were contractual difficulties and it took all of four days to resolve a certain point. My point was that the Beatles should in fact receive top billing on each occasion. This was contested vaguely by Sullivan who seemed to sense the importance or coming importance of the Beatles but who rejected my view that they were going to be the biggest thing in the world. His producer – a friend of ours now – has told me since that he told Sullivan that it was 'ridiculous' to give me top billing because a group hadn't made it big in the States for a long, long time and certainly not an English group.

However, we got our top billing and I returned to England with these contracts.

I came back to England delighted and excited and told the Beatles what was to come. They were pleased because they learned that one of the shows was from the Deauville Hotel in Miami, Florida, which meant that they would have a very pleasant few days in the sunshine. In fact they did have a small holiday there, but by the time they arrived the Beatles were so hot in America that I agreed to do the Carnegie Hall show and also a very big concert in Washington DC. So their planned holiday was brief.

On 7 February, they arrived at Kennedy International Airport to the sensational welcome from 10,000 fans.

As we waited until the passengers got off the plane and the four Beatles made their first appearance on American soil, there was a tumult of wild screams and applause from a fantastic crowd.

It seemed the entire building – the whole of the top of the airport – was filled with people. It was tremendously exciting and one of the most memorable moments of my life. I have never before or since seen so many photographers lined up anywhere in the world, except perhaps when the Beatles actually returned to England from the American tour.

From then on it was crowd scenes, wild demonstrations and that extraordinary 'We Love You Beatles' song, from New York to Washington. There were vast seas of faces in front of the Plaza. American DJs were on the phone by the minute, and the Beatles were beside themselves with delight and amazement. I had a suite on the twelfth floor of the Plaza Hotel, and it seemed that even from the moment I got there this room was filled with people, all talking, all selling, all buying, all very much in business with me and my Beatles.

This was my first experience actually of the extraordinary number of telephone calls which come to any hotel where I am staying when on tour with the Beatles.

If radio interest in the Beatles in the US was hysterical and youthful out of all proportion to the ages of the DJs, then press interest was no less extensive. Tens of thousands of words were written in serious newspapers and magazines, and searching attempts were made by star writers to probe the immediacy of the Beatles' success.

In the *Saturday Evening Post*, Vance Packard wrote:

The Beatles – under Mr. Epstein's tutelage – have put stress on filling other subconscious needs of teenagers. As restyled, they are no longer roughnecks but rather lovable, almost cuddly, imps. With their collarless jackets and boyish grins, they have succeeded in bringing out the mothering instinct in many adolescent girls.

The subconscious need that they fill most expertly is in taking adolescent girls clear out of this world. The youngsters in the darkened audiences can let go all inhibitions in a quite primitive sense when the Beatles cut loose. They can retreat from rationality and individuality. Mob pathology takes over, and they are momentarily freed of all of civilization's restraints.

The Beatles have become peculiarly adept at giving girls this release. Their relaxed, confident manner, their wild appearance, their whooping and jumping, their electrified rock-'n'-roll pulsing out into the darkness makes the girls want to jump and then scream. The more susceptible soon faint or develop twitching hysteria. (One reason why Russia's totalitarian leaders frown on rock-'n'-roll and jazz is that these forms offer people release from controlled behavior.)

In the same edition the bearded, questing Alfred Aronowitz followed the Beatles from New York to Miami and described his first impressions thus:

Amid a fanfare of screeches, there emerged four young Britons in Edwardian four-button suits. One was short and thick-lipped. Another was handsome and peach-fuzzed. A third had a heavy face and the hint of buck-teeth. On the fourth, the remnants of adolescent pimples were noticeable. Their names were Ringo Starr, Paul McCartney, John Lennon and George Harrison, but they were otherwise indistinguishable beneath their manes of mop-like hair.

Later in his article he wrote:

In the United States, Capitol Records, which has first rights to any E.M.I, release, originally turned down the Beatles' records. As the craze grew it not only issued them but poured $50,000 into a promotion campaign. 'Sure there was a lot of hype,' says Capitol vice president Voyle Gilmore. 'But all the hype in the world isn't going to sell a bad product.'

Nevertheless, that hype helped stir the interest of thousands of fans who greeted the Beatles at Kennedy Airport. Many thousands more waited for them at New York's Plaza Hotel. Outside the hotel, stacked up against barricades, the mob chanted 'We want the Beatles! We want the Beatles!' According to one maid, the Beatles found three girls hiding in their bathtub. Dozens of others climbed the fire exit to the 12th-floor wing in which the Beatles' entourage had been ensconced. Still others, with the names and pocketbooks of prominent families, checked in at the hotel and tried to get to the Beatles via the elevators.

On the 12th floor the Beatles rested in their suite while the phones rang with requests for interviews and autographs. One call was from a man who wanted to produce Beatle ashtrays. Another was from a promoter in Hawaii who wanted to book the Beatles.

Telegrams came in by the handful, and boxes loaded with fan mail.

My new American secretary and I coped as best we could with an indescribable volume of interest which poured into the hotel by cable, telephone and personal representation. I could not believe what was happening around me. Of course, it is part of life now, but at that time it seemed as if the whole Beatle business was almost beyond control.

It was and still is impossible to attend in detail to every single enquiry about the Beatles because it is not an overstatement to say that the whole world wants the Beatles. And in America it seemed that every American wanted them. It was marvellously exciting but the strain was immense.

On the Tuesday after the *Sullivan Show* the Beatles went by train in a snowstorm to Washington to perform to 8,000 people. They had intended to fly of course, not because they enjoy flying but because it is the only way to conserve time. Snow, however, prevented the flight, and after a very frightening and violent fight to the station through hysterical crowds, they attempted to relax on the train for their first visit – and mine – to the American capital.

I was looking forward to the visit because I felt I might be able to absorb some sense of American history as an antidote to the 1964 Beatle-type tumult of New York.

In fact, neither the Beatles nor I had much opportunity to see Washington because if anything it was wilder than

New York. The reception at the British Embassy was given by the British Ambassador Sir David Ormsby-Gore, later Lord Harlech, and his very charming wife.

Both Lord and Lady Harlech are extremely nice English people but, as is so often the way, their friends and guests were not quite as pleasant as the hosts, and the Beatles loathed the reception, the people, the atmosphere, the attitudes and since then they have refused practically every invitation of this type because they know what happens.

And what happens is that the Beatles, who are originally invited to see and to be seen, to hear and to be heard, to enjoy and to be enjoyed, become, in fact, simply autographing-automatons and a butt and a receptacle for every type of challenge, insult, demand and query imaginable and that, when the guests believe themselves to be important or very significant young Englishmen with marvellous educations, can be extremely difficult and unpleasant.

What happened at the embassy was that Ringo had a lock of his hair snipped off, that John was told 'Sign this' by a pink-faced young Britisher and said 'No', which I thought quite justifiable but the response from the Englishman was 'You'll sign this and like it'. 'Oh,' said John, and he left the reception and went home in a considerable temper. Ringo, Paul, George and I stuck it a little longer, buffeted, pulled and pushed, and only left when the writer's cramp became too much to bear.

Lord and Lady Harlech were very sorry and said so to the British press, who reported the event in full on their front pages. If we made a few friends at the British Embassy we made millions on the air through the wild hysterical comedian of American Radio. I was incredibly overwhelmed by the high-pressure salesmanship of Americans and by the techniques that they employ generally in gaining news and interviews and tapes.

I cannot say that I admired this enormously but nevertheless it was there and it was something which was quite stunning in its way. Since the visit, numerous attempts have been made to produce interviews, long-playing records which are not legal and which our lawyers have dealt with fairly severely, but it was interesting to notice that even the road manager, the transport managers and anyone else in any way involved with the Beatles were devoured by the DJs and by the interviewers for their views. This has since become a feature of Beatleism – that it is considered an asset to have some contact with someone who knows the Beatles. One of my staff tells me that his father was asked for an autograph not of the Beatles but of his own because he was the father of a member of the staff which was connected with the Beatles. Tenuous, but, in the extraordinary context of the Beatles, quite everyday.

America taught the Beatles one lesson and that was not to be taken for a ride if they could possibly help it – and if they were, to make it as gentle a ride as possible. The DJs – the folk heroes of the airwaves – had them in the palms of their microphones on the first tour.

The Beatles and the road managers could be secured for a handshake to say anything at all to a microphone. Paul would say 'And listen to the 1, 2, 3 Show, it's the greatest', and John would say 'Listen to the 3, 4, 5 Show, it's the most', and Malcolm Evans, the road manager, likewise. With four, strong, temperamental people like the Beatles and the lively young men around them, it was difficult to convince them that what they were doing was promoting commercial enterprises, not only without any reward but without any discernment or discrimination.

The DJs had a grand time but within a few days I had to stop it very severely. This warning was heeded and now they themselves refuse at all times to do promotions or to isolate one product from another, whether it is a commercial radio station or a toy balloon. It is extraordinary that the Beatles were taken in for so long, but then America is the land of the hard sell and their sales resistance at that time was not as strong as it is now. Now it is the strongest and most solid block of sales resistance in the world, and it is just as well because everyone in the world has something to sell to the Beatles, and not always are the products very good.

One of the problems of organising the lives of pop artistes and planning their careers is that interest must be sustained even when the artistes are not in the country, or on television, or on radio in person. The difficulty is how to maintain disc sales without personal appearances. I was not at all sure that when the Beatles left America interest could be maintained, although the DJs promised that because the Beatles were so good they would keep up the output and activity on their behalf.

I need not have worried. When 'Can't Buy Me Love', their sixth hit record, was released in America it went immediately into the number-one position, topping five other Beatle discs which had previously occupied the first five places in the charts. Thus one group occupied all six places and we knew that when we next entered the USA by the back door – that is through San Francisco – we were going to be a sensation, and the challenge and the responsibility was a little frightening. We learned that a ticker-tape welcome was planned and the Beatles – not being demonstrative people and still maintaining a sort of bland modesty – wondered whether this was quite the thing for them.

We decided to agree to the open-car drive through this very beautiful city because, we argued, it was part of show business.

Our recollections of the first American tour still dominate what has happened since November 1962, when the first Beatles record was issued. For although there had been many important events – chief among which was the royal premiere of the Beatles' first film in July this year in London – and though the Australasian tour was, in terms of crowd numbers, wilder and bigger than the American reception, there is, undeniably, something about the USA which exceeds every other nation in practically every respect.

We knew that America would make us or break us as world stars.

In fact, she made us.

2

Beginnings

I was expelled from Liverpool College at the age of ten, and though my parents found this most unamusing, at that age I was not greatly worried, for Liverpool College was not the last school in the world, nor, certainly, was it one of the best.

My expulsion was 'for inattention and for being below standard'. My parents were sent for and unfolded before them were my failings, itemised one by one in that catalogue-of-crime manner which comes so naturally to schoolmasters.

The housemaster explained that there would be no point in my remaining at a school in which I obviously had no pride, and he produced, as evidence of my unworthiness, a design for a programme which I had prepared beneath my desk in mathematics classes. It was decorated with dancing girls and, for a boy of ten, it was a fair piece of creative art, though it had nothing to do with mathematics.

I remember thinking that the mathematics master showed little imagination or appreciation when he discovered the programme. 'What, Epstein,' he thundered, 'is this piece of rubbishy nonsense?' and I said: 'A design, sir.'

'Rubbish and muck and girls,' he answered and threw me out of the classroom on the first of a series of short, sharp journeys which jerked and jolted me finally to a sofa in my home sitting opposite my father who said, with great justification and dwindling patience: 'I just don't know what on earth we're going to do with you.'

Nor did I and it was another fifteen years before I showed any real promise. I must surely be one of the latest developers of all time, for not until my mid-twenties did any pattern or purpose emerge in my life. If Keats had waited as long as I did to get going he wouldn't have written more than a couple of poems before his death.

My parents despaired many times over the years and I don't blame them, for throughout my schooldays I was one of those out-of-sorts boys who never quite fit. Who are ragged, nagged and bullied, and beloved of neither boys nor masters.

At the age of ten I had already been to three schools and had liked none of them.

I am an elder son – a hallowed position in a Jewish family – and much was to be expected of me. My father, Harry, son of a Polish migrant, naturally sought in me some sign of an adequate heir to the family business, but, alas, he scarcely saw a sign of any quality at all beyond a loyalty to the family, which, thanks to the steadfastness of my parents, has not faltered.

I was born in a nursing home on 19 September 1934, in Rodney Street, Liverpool. This is the Harley Street of the city – a wide and rather magnificent road of tall, old houses bearing brass plates and learned names, and it was as good a start in life as you could get in Liverpool, which is not, conventionally, a very beautiful city.

My mother, Queenie, still the loveliest woman I know, was intensely proud that her first-born was a boy, and when, twenty-one months later, my brother Clive arrived, the Epsteins looked like being a happy and promising little family unit.

Today, thirty years later, this is so again, but there were many intervening spans of misunderstanding, failure and unhappiness before we found real contentment as a family. I was not the best of sons and I was certainly the worst of pupils.

My first school was a kindergarten in Liverpool where I hammered wooden shapes through a plywood board and made rather a mess of it. I constructed models from cardboard and they wouldn't stick. And, after a lethargic fashion, I learned to read and to write.

When I was six, Hitler, who had become rather a nuisance, launched a sustained attempt to destroy Liverpool, and though we lived several miles from the vulnerable docks target, our Childwall suburb became too close for comfort and safety.

Thousands of Liverpool children were evacuated to the country and separated from their parents, but other families decided to close up their homes in the city and move as units either across the Mersey to the sanctuary of the Wirral peninsular, or up the coast to Southport, where there was a substantial Jewish community.

My father chose Southport and we stayed there until the bombing was over. I was put into Southport College where I made my first fumbling attempt at drawing and design which I enjoyed hugely. But away from the protective warmth of a kindergarten and experiencing for the first time the alien discipline of teachers with an eye on potential scholarship candidates, I began to realise that with little to offer in the way of brilliance and nothing in the way of acceptable personality, I was not a very popular individual.

A tiny child in a well-adjusted family doesn't know too much about popularity or outside relationships. He has his parents and they love him and that is that.

But as a growing boy I discovered that I was not very good at forming friendships. Indeed, I believe I am not especially successful at it now, though it is easier these days because I am probably a nicer person.

And, of course, today there is another factor in my placing with other people – I wield a certain amount of what, for want of a better word, is described as power. This in turn brings other problems because it is no longer easy to know whether I am wanted for what I am or for what I am supposed to have in terms of material goods or power. In other words – do people want me or do they want the Beatles through me?

The bombing, in 1943, appeared to be over and my family returned to Childwall. I was taken from Southport College, and after an interview with the headmaster of

Liverpool College, I was admitted as a scholar of whom they expected no great brilliance.

In this, the stern and upright men who controlled this minor public school were not disappointed for I was, as I say, expelled. Expulsion is an ugly word and I had always believed that it only happened to bullies or thieves or liars like Flashman in *Tom Brown's Schooldays*, a sombre book which I had read without enthusiasm.

But I was not a bully – I was far too slight and cowardly. I was not a thief, for my parents gave me most of what I wanted, probably a little more than I needed, and I had little chance to lie because I hardly ever spoke to anyone.

I left Liverpool College without regret.

One feature of life which I experienced there and at other schools, and sometimes since, was anti-Semitism. Even now it lurks round the corner in some guise or other, and though it doesn't matter to me any more, it did when I was young.

Lightly though I took my dismissal from Liverpool College, I still had to make a pretence at formal education, but my parents were running short of ideas. My father, an uncomplicated man, had been a solid and successful grammar-school boy and he found it difficult to know why I was so wretched a pupil.

Obviously, an expellee from Liverpool College would not be readily accepted at my father's old school, Liverpool Collegiate, or at the other major grammar school, Liverpool Institute (which, many years later, attempted to educate two of the Beatles – and almost succeeded). Good grammar schools don't want public-school rejects.

So I was sent to a private school whose mentors asked no questions and from which my parents swiftly subtracted me after a few weeks because it was so thoroughly unsatisfactory.

It was in Liverpool and it was so awful that, sorry though my parents were to part with me, they decided that I would have to go away to school – to board. The problem was that they and their advisers were running out of schools.

Well ... when in doubt turn to the religion you know. Thus was I despatched with my tuck box and a headful of good advice to a Jewish prep school called Beaconsfield near Tunbridge Wells. This I enjoyed a little better and I took up horse riding and art, both of which I did pretty well. I began to feel a little more at evens with the world and I made friends with a little horse called Amber, who got on very well with Jews.

But ... I was approaching the age of thirteen, which meant that I should sit examinations for a public school, and these I failed on a majestic scale.

I had, by now, developed a conscious hatred of formal education. I was bad at mathematics and all sciences. I had no rapport with the men teaching me, nor, I felt, had they any sympathy with my difficulties. One by one, as examination followed interview and interview followed examination, the great public schools of England turned me down – Rugby and Repton and Clifton and, no doubt, others.

So once again my parents were faced with the problem of keeping my knees beneath a desk until I was, at least, legally able to leave school. They solved it, as many patient paters and maters before and since have solved it, by sending me to one of those benevolent academies where failures are welcomed although not accepted as such, and protected almost to manhood.

This one was in Dorset. Games were considered to be rather special and I played rugby under coercion and not very well, but I suffered it with calm, and in the evenings I pursued my interest in design and colour. Art was not then considered to be a worthy occupation for a red-blooded son of an Englishman, but it was the only thing in my narrow world for which I cared. Also it was the only thing at which I was any good.

Back in Liverpool, my father who was, and is, a proud citizen and father, was writing and working hard to find me a good school before it was too late.

Finally he succeeded, and in the autumn of 1948 just after my fourteenth birthday, my parents and brother telephoned me in Dorset to say that I was going to Wrekin College in Shropshire, a well-known public school with a reputation for producing executives and successful leaders of one kind or another, though not of a level of Eton or Harrow.

But the vision of its spartan rigidity beckoned me not at all, so 'Oh' I said, and at the end of the year I wrote with gloomy pessimism, 'Now for the Wrekin I hate. I am going there only because my parents want me to ... it is a pity because it has been a great year for me. The birth of new ideas. A little more popularity.'

A little later, I wrote – and I repeat it now with wry

hindsight – 'Just before my first day at Wrekin we spent a day at Sheffield – my mother's home city. I expected to be taken to the Grand. But no.'

The Grand is a large, expensive hotel – the biggest in Sheffield – and it is curious that even in those days I expressed my disappointment at not being taken there. Now, on a wider, more discriminating and rather more expensive scale, I still find little pleasure in accepting less than the best, and it may be this leaning towards superlative which drove me on in business and will continue to whip me into fresh activity.

Well, Wrekin came and went. I didn't like it nor it me and the school report said: 'Could do better', or 'Listless effort this term', and I think they may have been right. Except in two respects: I had become a good painter and a reasonable amateur actor. I played in the normal school one-acters and I found I enjoyed speaking lines.

In art I came top of the form and I was glad because although I had accepted defeat in a very wide range of subjects, I had always wanted to be best at something. And on the basis of proficiency with paint and paper, at the age of sixteen, and before sitting for what was then the School Certificate examination, I wrote home and asked to be taken away from school so that I could become a dress designer.

This caused a great deal of distress. The masters at Wrekin naturally thought it was ruinous to leave school without a single qualification and there was, to their minds, nothing less manly than dress designing.

My father agreed, and he had an additional anxiety, for

he believed such a job would not only not pay enough, but, worse, could lead me into unemployment. Thus, I did not become one.

Although I knew good design from bad, though I could create dresses and draw them, though to be a dress designer was all I wanted to be, I went – in that curiously illogical way of the son and heir – into the family business for which I neither cared nor in which I expected to succeed.

Still ... if you had been to seven schools, had a rotten time in all of them, been expelled from one and thwarted from your single aim, you can be relied upon to accept anything, and so, on 10 September 1950, aged nearly sixteen, thin, curly-haired, pink-cheeked and half educated, I reported for duty in the family furniture store in Walton, Liverpool.

3

Strife

My starting pay as a furniture salesman was £5 a week, which seemed quite a lot, and the day after I joined the business I sold a £12 dining table to a woman who had come into the shop for a mirror.

It was a pleasurable experience, not because I wanted the woman to part with money she should have spent on a mirror, but because I honestly felt she would be better off with a dining table.

This is a principle I have applied in business since, because I believe that it is a salesman's job. The buyer must be convinced that what he wanted would not be good for him and that what he does not want would be very good for him.

I became a good salesman and I surprised my father and I believe we were both rather proud.

Day by day I began to enjoy procuring other people's confidence – watching them relax and show trust in me. It was pleasurable to see the wary look dissolve, to know that they believed that good things were ahead for them and that I would be the provider.

This is not to be pompous; it is, I believe, the essence of successful and honourable salesmanship.

I developed into a relaxed seller and, consequently, more of an Epstein, for we were very much a business family, though, I hope, never a greedy one. Finding the job easy allowed me more time to have a hard look at the layout of the store – at the design and the colour schemes and at the products themselves. I was, and still am, very interested in the way things should be displayed and I have a self-devouring passion for quality.

In those days, the Walton store was not exactly a candidate for a design award. Our window displays were, I thought, rather awful and I horrified the conventional furniture men by doing outrageous things with the pieces.

I placed chairs in the windows with their backs to the window-shoppers. Backs of chairs in view? Unheard of! Yet in every home you see the backs of chairs in the fireside pattern ... indeed, you cannot enter a room without seeing the back of a chair.

I was very keen on splayed legs. They were just on the way in at that time, because slowly the post-war austerity hangover was diminishing and sellers and buyers were reluctant to return to the ugliness of the 1930-ish design.

New young men with degrees in Art were discarding moquette, stripping the curls and twirls from sideboards and chairs, and bringing in clean lines and new fabrics. White became an 'in' colour, wallpaper became fashionable again, and everywhere that was anywhere, suddenly, there were splayed legs! I was entranced by the possibilities.

My father, not convinced that I wasn't running before I could stand but also thrilled to see me settling to something at last, decided to have me apprenticed to a city furnishing store – the Times, in Lord Street, Liverpool.

I worked there for six months, still on £5 a week, but I was beginning to feel that I was worth a good deal more. Still, I learned a lot about window-dressing and very much more about people and their desire to be convinced and persuaded. As a reward for my work, the Times gave me a Parker pen and pencil, the first of which, many years later, I loaned to Paul McCartney to sign his first contract with me.

Of course, I often needed more money and when I was hard up I asked my father for a pound or two. He always met my requests but I hated asking. That I loathed profoundly, and though I shall never again have to seek money from anyone, I have a deeply imprinted recollection of the unpleasant moment when one has to say ... 'I am a little short of cash. Could you possibly lend me some?'

Honourably discharged from the Times, I returned to the Walton store with another new suit and here I was, I thought, developing into a worthy inheritor of a stable, profitable business which I had learned to like.

I was settling down; the designing of the store was becoming my own responsibility, and all in all, my mother and father were really quite pleased with their Brian. The future seemed firm and bright and assured.

But, on 9 December 1952, a letter came from a grim

and grey and joyless office in Parnall Square, off Renshaw Street, Liverpool, to tell the pleased-with-himself young son and heir that he was to present himself for a medical examination to ascertain his medical fitness for the army.

I was appalled and shocked though I shouldn't have been since this two-year punishment was then a routine, predictable segment of teenage life. I viewed it as a wasteful gulf but, in fact, for me it turned out to be immeasurably worse than that. For if I had been a poor schoolboy, I was surely the lousiest soldier in the world, not excepting the sad, demented creatures who bianco their trousers and eat their webbing belts in their attempts to fiddle a discharge. I passed the medical which, apart from a cough or two, was not, I felt, very stringent, and I applied to join the RAF because I believed it would be easier than the army. But with the quaint logic of the armed forces, I was allocated to the army, as a clerk in the Royal Army Service Corps. Basic training was at Aldershot, and if there is a more depressing place than this in all Europe, then I would not be interested to know of it.

It was like a prison and it was squalid and meaningless. It was cold and hostile and I did everything wrong. I turned right instead of left, and turned about instead of at ease, and if I was told just to stand still, then I fell over.

I entered 1953 in a mood of immovable pessimism and I was not cheered by evidence that most of the lads with me were taking their hardship with fortitude. Several of the public-schoolboys who had shared my moans in the first few weeks were snatched away to become officer-cadets but naturally – for the army is not always wrong – I was not included.

I cannot imagine anything worse for morale than Lieutenant Epstein in charge of a platoon of men under heavy mortar fire.

The year 1953 was, of course, the year of the Coronation, and though I was a rotten soldier I had a perverse wish to be on parade in London that day. I suppose it was the splendid stage-management and the majesty of the thing, but I wasn't nearly good enough to be used so I went out of barracks and got very drunk instead – after a tour of pubs and clubs which left me with three-halfpence and a disagreeable headache.

My failure to be selected as an officer did not, however, prevent me from impersonating officers and one night this involved me in trouble.

I had deviously secured a posting to Regent's Park barracks and I used to enjoy off-duty life in the West End for I had a lot of relatives in London. On this particular night I had myself brought back to camp in a large car. It slid gently to a halt outside the barracks' gate. I marched into camp wearing – rather pompously I'm afraid – a bowler, pinstriped suit and, over my arm, an umbrella.

The guard saluted me and the guard commander saluted me and two wretched convicted deserters, wearing denims and carrying buckets, jerked their heads in an Eyes Right. Also, a myopic clerk, who worked at the next desk by day, peered at me and said: 'Good night, sir.' All of which I allowed to pass by without a murmur one way or the other.

The orderly officer did none of these things. He came from behind a whitewashed wall like a cat, and marching into the baleful yellow glow from the guardroom, he barked: 'Private Epstein. You will report to the company office at 10.00 hours tomorrow morning charged with impersonating an officer.'

I was kept in barracks for some days – not for the first time. This, for me, was the worst punishment because it deprived me of my only compensation – the freedom of London after 6 p.m. And within ten months of joining the army, my nerves became seriously upset.

I reported to the barracks doctor who seemed quite alarmed, and after a long, fruitless talk about my problems and the need for 'facing-up' and 'pulling myself together', he referred me to a psychiatrist.

The first one spent several hours discussing my early life and my schooldays and then, as is the way with doctors, he sought a second opinion. A third and fourth opinion followed and with remarkable unity they decided that I was a compulsive civilian and quite unfit for military service. I was no use to the army nor it to me, with which view I readily agreed.

After less than twelve months as the most unsatisfactory private soldier in the Royal Army Service Corps, I was discharged on medical grounds though in that quaintly detached and benevolent way which sets the army aside from reality, I have a military reference which describes me as a sober, reliable and conscientious soldier.

I ran like a hare for the Euston train after handing in my hideous uniform and I arrived in Liverpool prepared

Regent's Park Barracks,
Albany Street,
London N.W.1.

Date: **2 7** Jan 54.

<u>S/22739590 Pte Epstein B. R.A.S.C.</u>

Extract from AF B 2066 (Annual Report
and Employment Sheet).

Documentation Clerk –   'A concientious and hard working
clerk who uses his initiative and
can in every respect be depended
upon to see a job through
satisfactorily without supervision.
Of smart appearance and sober habits
at all times, he is utterly
trustworthy.'

Certified correct:

34 Personnel Section R.A.S.C.

to return, to my parents and Clive, as a junior executive anxious to work very hard.

They welcomed me generously though they were very worried about the discharge and to my great relief I felt instantly at home back in the furniture store in Walton.

There was, in the store, a tiny record department which I had helped to open, and though I was not musical, I was interested in good music and I loved classical records.

I had, by now, passed my driving test at the fourth attempt. I had the use of a car, and was earning much more than £5, there was a good record department and there were to be no more interruptions from the drill sergeant at Aldershot. I was, I believed, nicely settled.

But ... by night I was seeking escape in the cool and cultivated dusk of the front stalls of Liverpool Playhouse. This was, and always will be, a splendid repertory centre – the hothouse of Redgrave and Donat and Diana Wynyard in their beginning bloom ...

... And of Brian Bedford, the brilliant young medal-winner from RADA who had Liverpool reeling with his immense and powerful Hamlet.

Offstage, Bedford and a few other young optimists formed a clique including actors and actresses, designers and writers. Plus a settled, soon-to-be-stolid furniture salesman from Walton called Epstein who began to feel rather old.

One night, in the Basnett bar – an extremely pleasant pub, long and narrow and with a marble counter; a stage-whisper away from the Playhouse – a gang of us were having a drink after the show. It was Saturday – the final night of a three-week run – and Helen Lindsay, a lovely actress now well known on television, had done very well in a difficult part.

There was a lot of praise and noise and everyone was very pleased with themselves in that disarmingly vain way nicer actors have. I suddenly felt depressed and I said: 'I think I'll pop off home, I'm rather tired.'

Brian bawled: 'Nonsense. This is a wonderful night. We're only just starting.' I said: 'You may be – all of you. I'm a doomed middle-aged businessman.'

Helen said: 'What do you want to do with your life?' and I replied, to my immense surprise, 'I wouldn't mind being an actor. But it's too late.' Brian refused to accept this and said: 'There's a very good chance you could get into RADA.'

He had, of course, distinguished himself there and he and Helen encouraged me to seek an audition. I was to travel to London to meet the then Director, John Fernald. A few weeks later I arrived in London and, at the Academy, I met Fernald – a former Liverpool Playhouse Director – and performed two pieces for him. A short reading from Eliot's *Confidential Clerk*, and another from *Macbeth*.

I thought they were not particularly well done but Fernald, an agreeable and able man, said: 'That was not at all bad. Would you like, presuming you are suitable, to start next term?'

I liked very much and once again I left my tables and chairs in Walton and set off South. My parents, who had been forced to accept the interruption of the army, were very unhappy about the latest break in my career. They believed that becoming an actor was only a shade better than my boyhood dreams of dress-designing. It was unstable and, like dress-designing, unmanly; there was no money in it. And who was to take over the family business? But their wonderful regard for my personal happiness persuaded them to let me become an actor.

Thus, at twenty-two, though already a secure and fairly successful businessman, I submitted myself once again to the discipline of community life. I became a student at the Royal Academy of Dramatic Art and dreamed of stardom and great fame.

RADA at that time was producing the young players who formed the new wave in the British theatre. O'Toole and Finney, Susannah York and Joanna Dunham. Joanna was in my class and she was one of the few people at RADA who made life bearable, for within a few weeks I grew to loathe the place and the other students, and I was, yet again, face-to-face with failure.

I stuck it three terms and discovered a distaste for the actor-type which lingers even now. The narcissism appalled me, and the detachment of the actor from other people and their problems left me quite amazed.

An actor is not the least interested in anyone else. He seeks the friendship of those in the business who have succeeded and those outside who can help him. He fears failure with an awful intensity and he will never associate with anyone who has failed in case he himself becomes contaminated. There are exceptions but they are few.

I think my disenchantment with the acting profession became total when I spent a fortnight in Stratford with the Royal Shakespeare people. They were really frightful, and I believe that nowhere could one discover such phoney relationships nor witness hypocrisy practised on so grand a scale, almost as an art.

So, after the end of my third term at RADA, I returned home for the vacation nursing a secret decision never to leave home again and hiding a sense of inadequacy which was almost complete. Was there, I wondered, no job I could stick for longer than a year?

The vacation over, I was due to start my fourth term. My parents took me for a farewell dinner to the Adelphi Hotel in Liverpool and asked me, purely as a matter of ritual: 'Are you quite sure you want to go back?'

'I don't want to,' I said. 'I want to stay here. I should like to come back into the business if I can.'

4

Discovery

When I left RADA I was determined to throw myself into the family business and make an increasing, and lifelong success of it. It was 1957 – I was twenty-three and full of resolve to do well for my own and my parents' sake.

My brother Clive had now joined the firm and my father hoped for great expansion. We opened a new store in Liverpool – our first in the city centre – and although there had been a record section in Walton which I had run, the new store in Charlotte Street was far more promising.

There was quite a large record section, I was placed in charge with one assistant and we started to do quite well. In Walton we had been fortunate to take £70 for records in a week's sale, but we took £20 on the first morning in Charlotte Street. Anne Shelton opened the store and we were away to a swinging start.

At that time, of course, I was only vaguely interested in popular music though I had always been a keen concert-goer. My favourite composer in those days was Sibelius, but in these changing times, he is now placed in my affections alongside Paul McCartney and John Lennon.

The Christmas which followed the opening became known in the record world as 'Mary's Boy Child' year. It was a massive seller and we were one of the few shops where the disc was always in stock. But this was only the beginning of our reputation for I was determined to be known as the record-dealer who had everything the customer wanted: hit songs, small-sellers, specialist records – the lot.

I established a foolproof system in showing when a record pile needed renewing. This meant we never ran out of any given disc.

I turned no one away with a 'Sorry. We don't have it.' If for instance a customer ordered 'The Birth of a Baby' on LP I would order not one but another for permanent stock, for I believed that one query was indicative of some sort of constant demand, and two or three queries suggested a potentially larger scale.

A few years later this policy was to change my life.

But for the time being, sales at Nems – North End Music Stores – were mounting and the staff increased slowly by twos and threes to an eventual thirty, all working very hard. I built up a best-seller list which I checked twice daily and from this I expanded the pop music department and pushed the classical discs upstairs. I put in ridiculously long hours, working from 8 a.m. until long into the night, and on Sundays I used to come into the store to make out orders.

In 1959, we opened another store, this time in the heart

of Liverpool's shopping centre. It was opened by Anthony Newley, then a very popular film actor and pop singer who, everyone knew, was going to be a great star. I had not met him before and although I was still shy of stars and anxious not to be a bore in their dressing rooms, I persuaded a Decca representative to introduce us.

Newley was an exceedingly friendly, diffident young man, very modest and easy-going, and we got on well. He agreed to open the store and spent a day with me and my family, just relaxing, without pretensions, and I recall thinking that this was how a real star should behave. In fact it is precisely the way my artistes behave, when they are permitted by press and public.

The traffic on opening day in Whitechapel was stopped by Newley. Central Liverpool had never seen such scenes except for a victorious Cup Final team, and the mood and varied ages of the fans suggested that pop-singing was becoming more than a passing three-week wonder.

Finally that day the road was closed and Newley was able to open the store into which, years later, on a Saturday afternoon, walked leather-jacketed Raymond Jones. And eighteen months after that, the traffic was stopped again – when the Beatles visited the store.

By autumn 1961 the store was running like an eighteen-jewelled watch. It was showing good returns and the ordering and stocking systems were so automatic that I was, once again, becoming a little restless and bored. Life was getting too easy. On Saturday, 28 October, I had just come back from a long holiday in Spain during which I had wondered how I could expand my interests.

And then, suddenly, though quite undramatically, a few words from Raymond Jones brought the solution. The words, of course, were 'Have you got a disc by the Beatles?'

I had never given a thought to any of the Liverpool beat groups then up and coming in cellar clubs. They were not part of my life, because I was out of the age group, and also because I had been too busy. But I knew that a lot of boys had taken up the guitar because of the influence of teenage stars since the early days of Presley and Tommy Steele, through the late fifties to the Shadows, who, by the autumn of 1961, were the star instrumental group backing Cliff Richard, unchallenged British pop idol.

The name 'Beatle' meant nothing to me though I vaguely recalled seeing it on a poster advertising a university dance at New Brighton Tower and I remembered thinking it was an odd and purposeless spelling.

Raymond Jones was one of any average dozen customers who called in daily for unknown discs and there seems now no valid reason why, beyond my normal efforts to satisfy a customer, I should have gone to such lengths to trace the actual recording artistes. But I did and I wonder sometimes whether there is not something mystically magnetic about the name 'Beatle'?

Now they are world-famous, the Beatles defy analysis as to the specific ingredients of their success but I do wonder whether they would have been quite as big if they had been called, for example, the Liverpool Four, or something equally prosaic.

One interesting feature of the Beatles' entry into my life was that, without being conscious of it, I had seen them many times in the store.

I had been bothered a little by the frequent visits of a group of scruffy lads in leather and jeans who hung around the store in the afternoons, chatting to the girls and lounging on the counters listening to records. They were pleasant enough boys, untidy and a little wild, and they needed haircuts.

I mentioned to the girls in the shop that I thought the youth of Liverpool might while their afternoons away somewhere else, but they assured me that the boys were well behaved and amusing and they occasionally bought records. Also, said the girls, they seemed to know good discs from bad.

Though I didn't know it, the four lads were the Beatles, filling in part of the long afternoon between the lunchtime and evening shows in the best cellars.

On 28 October Raymond Jones left the store after I had taken a note of his request. I wrote on a pad: '"My Bonnie". The Beatles. Check on Monday.'

But before I had had time to check on Monday, two girls came into the store and they too asked for a disc by this curiously spelled group. And this, contrary to legend, was the sum total of demand for the Beatles' disc at this time in Liverpool. It is untrue that there was a milling fighting crowd around Nems waiting for the disc to arrive.

That afternoon I telephoned a few of the agents who imported discs, told them what I was looking for and found that no one had heard of the thing, let alone imported it.

I might have stopped bothering there and then if I hadn't made it a rigid rule never to turn any customer away.

And I was sure there was something very significant in three queries for one unknown disc in two days.

I talked to contacts in Liverpool and found, which I hadn't realised, that the Beatles were in fact a Liverpool group, that they had just returned from playing in clubs in the seamy, seedy end of Hamburg where they were well known, successful and fairly impoverished. A girl I know said: 'The Beatles? They're the greatest. They're at the Cavern this week.' ... The Cavern. Formerly a jazz club which had been a huge success in the mid 1950s, it was now owned by Raymond McFall, an ex-accountant who was filling some of his jazz programmes with raw 'Made in Liverpool' beat music played, usually, on loudly amplified guitars and drums. The Cavern was a disused warehouse beneath Mathew Street, Liverpool, and I remember that I was apprehensive at the thought of having to march in there among a lot of teenagers who were dressed as if they belonged, talking teenage talk and listening to music only they understood. Also, I was not a member.

So I asked a girl to have a word with the Cavern, to say that I would like to pop in on 9 November at lunchtime and to ensure that I wasn't stopped at the door. I have never enjoyed scenes on doors with bouncers and people asking for 'your membership card, sir' or that sort of thing.

I arrived at the greasy steps leading to the vast cellar and descended gingerly past a surging crowd of beat fans to a desk where a large man sat examining membership cards. He knew my name and he nodded to an opening in the wall which led into the central of the three tunnels which make up the rambling Cavern.

Inside the club it was as black as a deep grave, dank and damp and smelly, and I regretted my decision to come. There were sometimes two hundred young people there jiving, chatting or eating a 'Cavern lunch' – soup, roll, Cokes and things. Over all the speakers were loudly amplified current hit discs, then mainly American, and I remember considering the possibility of some 'tie' between Nems and the Cavern in connection with the Top Twenty.

I started to talk to one of the girls. 'Hey,' she hissed. 'The Beatles're going on now.' And there on a platform at the end of the cellar's middle tunnel stood the four boys. Then I eased myself towards the stage, past rapt young faces and jigging bodies and for the first time I saw the Beatles properly.

They were not very tidy and not very clean. But they were tidier and cleaner than anyone else who performed at that lunchtime session or, for that matter, at most of the sessions I later attended. I had never seen anything like the Beatles on any stage. They smoked as they played and they ate and talked and pretended to hit each other. They turned their backs on the audience and shouted at them and laughed at private jokes.

But they gave a captivating and honest show and they had very considerable magnetism. I loved their ad libs and I was fascinated by this, to me, new music with its pounding bass beat and its vast engulfing sound. There was quite clearly an excitement in the otherwise unpleasing dungeon which was quite removed from any of the formal entertainments provided at places like the Liverpool Empire or the London Palladium, though I learned later that the response to the Beatles was falling off a little in Liverpool – they, like me, were becoming bored because they could see no great progress in their lives.

I hadn't appreciated it but I was something of a figure in the Liverpool Pop Scene as a Director of Nems, and I was surprised when, after the Beatles had finished, Bob Wooler, the Cavern Disc Jockey, who later became a great friend of mine, announced over the loudspeaker that Mr Epstein of Nems was in the Cavern and would the kids give me a welcome.

This sort of announcement then, as now, embarrassed me and I was a little diffident when I reached the stage to try to talk to the Beatles about 'My Bonnie'.

George was the first to talk to me. A thin pale lad with a lot of hair and a very pleasant smile. He shook hands and said, 'Hello there. What brings Mr Epstein here?' and I explained that I'd had queries about their German disc.

He called the others over – John, Paul and Peter Best – and said, 'This man would like to hear our disc.'

Paul looked pleased and went into the tiny band room next to the stage to get it played. I thought it was good, but nothing very special. I stayed in the Cavern and heard the second half of the programme and found myself liking the Beatles more and more. There was some indefinable charm there. They were extremely amusing and, in a rough 'take it or leave' way, very attractive.

Never in my life had I thought of managing an artiste or

representing one, or being in any way involved in behind-the-scenes presentation, and I will never know what made me say to this eccentric group of boys that I thought a further meeting might be helpful to them and to me.

But something must have sparked between us because I arranged a meeting at the Whitechapel store at 4.30 p.m. on 3 December 1961, 'just for a chat', I explained, without mentioning management, because nothing as precise as that had yet formed in my mind.

5

No!

In the intervening days I sold over a hundred copies of 'My Bonnie', and after the initial success, sales snowballed and the record went quite well for a first effort in a provincial city.

December 3rd arrived but at 4.30 p.m. there were only three Beatles. Paul was the missing one and after half an hour of listless conversation – for it was pointless to talk any sort of terms with only three of them – I asked George to ring Paul and find out why he was late.

George returned from the phone with a half-smile which annoyed me a little and said, 'Paul's just got up and he is having a bath.' I said, 'This is disgraceful, he's very late,' and George, with his slow, lopsided smile, said, 'And very clean.' Paul arrived an hour later and we all went to a milk bar. We had a coffee each and I found that they had no management – or guidance beyond their instincts – those uncanny instincts on which I now rely so much.

They were very respectful to me but I didn't know whether this was because I had money, a car and a record shop, or whether it was because they liked me. I suspect it was a little of both.

The five of us discussed, in vague terms, contracts and their futures, but of course none of us knew anything about the right terms or the prices for their sort of act.

We left the milk bar with nothing decided except that we would have another meeting the following Wednesday and in the meantime I went to see a Liverpool lawyer friend, Rex Makin, to discuss management and to try to share some of my excitement about the Beatles. Makin, who had known me well for years, said, 'Oh, yes, another Epstein idea. How long before you lose interest in this one?' A justifiable comment but one which offended me because I felt strongly and irrationally that I was going to be permanently involved with the Beatles.

One of my earliest feelings about their work was that they were so badly paid. They earned 75/- each per night at the Cavern and that was above the normal rate and was, in fact, more than Ray McFall need have paid them. I found later that he had insisted on increasing their pay because he too felt there was more than ordinary talent there, and consequently greater drawing power for him at the Cavern.

I believe very strongly in the rewarding of ability and I hoped that even if I were not to run their affairs completely I could at least secure a decent rate for their performances. But first I had to be sure that they were reliable people. I asked around the Cavern about them and tried to form a picture of them – of their reputation, their reliability and so on.

Not everyone to whom I spoke was in favour of these unruly lads who had thought more of their guitars than their GCE and who had spent a lot of time in sinful Hamburg. One man, still a talkative colourful figure on the Liverpool Scene, was very direct. I was in a club in the city, called the Jacaranda, talking about the upsurge beat music which had taken me so much by surprise, and I said to this man: 'Do you know a group called the Beatles?'

'Do I? Listen, Brian,' he said, 'I know the Beatles very well indeed. Too well. My advice to you – and I know something about the pop world – is to have nothing to do with them. They will let you down.'

He was more wrong than anyone will ever know. For not only have the Beatles never let me down, or anyone else down since I met them, they have always done far more than their contracts demanded and would have been hurt if some things had been written into their contracts. They, like me, prefer some things to be taken on trust.

On the Wednesday before I again asked them to come to the shop, it was early closing, and I met them outside the door in Whitechapel and led them in. I looked at them all slowly and said: 'Quite simply, you need a manager. Would you like me to do it?' No one spoke for a moment or two and then John, in a low husky voice, blurted: 'Yes.'

The others nodded. Paul, gazing in that disturbingly wide-eyed way, asked, 'Will it make much difference to us? I mean it won't make any difference to the way we play.'

'Course it won't. I'm very pleased anyway,' I said

without the slightest idea of the disappointments ahead before I could contemplate taking a penny in manager's fees. I started with the Beatles as I have with all my artistes – running them at a loss until they earn enough to afford to lose a percentage.

We all sat and looked at one another for a moment or two, none of us really knowing what to say next. Then John broke the silence: 'Right then, Brian. Manage us, now. Where's the contract? I'll sign it.'

I had no idea what a contract even looked like and I didn't think it would be sensible to take the signatures of four teenagers on any old piece of paper. So I sent away for a sample contract and produced it at our next meeting on the following Sunday at the Casbah, a beat club at the home of Pete Best, then, of course, the Beatles' drummer.

The contract had been drawn up by people who knew more about a fast buck than does a slow doe. I thought it an inhuman document providing simply for the enslavement of any artiste eager and gullible enough to place his name over a stamp. Its like is still around and there are several artistes, some of them quite well known, bound by this form of contract. I am not permitted to name them but they and their owners know who they are.

However, using it as a guide for wording, and by modifying and adapting the terms, we eventually drew up a Beatles–Epstein agreement which each Beatle signed in the presence of Alastair Taylor, then employed in the shop, now Nems's General Manager. One signature was never placed on that first contract. Mine. But I abided by the terms and no one worried.

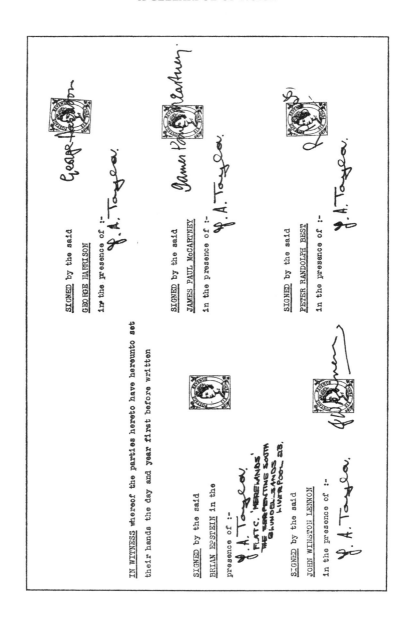

IN WITNESS whereof the parties hereto have hereunto set their hands the day and year first before written

SIGNED by the said
BRIAN EPSTEIN in the
presence of :-
J. A. Taylor.
FLAT C. 'MERE LANDS'
THE SERPENTINE SOUTH
BLUNDELLSANDS
LIVERPOOL 23.

SIGNED by the said
JOHN WINSTON LENNON
in the presence of :-
J. A. Taylor.

SIGNED by the said
GEORGE HARRISON
in the presence of :-
J. A. Taylor.

SIGNED by the said
JAMES PAUL McCARTNEY
in the presence of :-
J. A. Taylor.

SIGNED by the said
PETER RANDOLPH BEST
in the presence of :-
J. A. Taylor.

I felt that having now to guide the career of these four trusting boys, I should make it a priority matter to persuade a recording executive to hear them sing and play. I wanted someone from one of the big companies, preferably Decca, because I had better personal contacts with the sales people there.

Mike Smith of Decca came to the Cavern in December 1961, and caused a tremendous stir. What an occasion! An A & R (Artistes and Repertoire) manager at the Cavern!

I had approached him through a Liverpool representative of Decca, and I found him very helpful and friendly. We had dinner and at the Cavern he was 'knocked out' by the Beatles. He thought that they were tremendous and this made me very elated because he was at the centre of the music business and his word, I thought therefore, carried authority.

I said nothing to the boys about this at first because I wanted to calm down, but when I did tell them they became very excited and we all felt more confident. Wanting to behave like a manager I approached Ray McFall and said, 'How about more bookings for the Beatles?'

He said he would do what he could, and I was very proud when Bob Wooler came to me one day and asked, 'What are the Beatles doing on Sunday?' I reached for my diary and said: 'They may be busy but I will try and fit you in.' This, at last, was being a manager and I remember the occasion vividly.

The big groups in Liverpool in those days were the Undertakers, Johnny Sandon and the Searchers, Rory Storme and the Hurricanes (this group had a drummer called Ringo), the Remo Four, the Four Jays (later to be known as the Fourmost), the Big Three, and the very promising Gerry and the Pacemakers. I was sure that the Beatles would leave many of them behind in a very short time.

Mike Smith agreed, and we secured them an audition at Decca on New Year's Day 1962. They came to London and stayed at the Royal Hotel, paying 27/- a night for bed and breakfast in Woburn Place. They were poor and I wasn't rich but we all celebrated with rum and with Scotch and Coke which was becoming a Beatle drink.

We were gently excited – although we knew that a recording test was only the beginning. We knew also – from the boys' experience in Hamburg, from mine in the retail trade – that of the hundreds of songs which are sifted from the tens of thousands submitted, only a few score would become hits.

And we were not even on tape with our songs!

I said to the boys the following morning: 'What if the whole thing collapses? There's no guarantee we can get near a contract yet. Will you be very disappointed?' They all said: 'No.' But their faces said 'Yes' and I realised that I had been building up ridiculously high hopes on the recording test.

At 11 a.m. on 1 January we arrived at Decca in a thin bleak wind, with snow and ice afoot. Mike Smith was late and we were pretty annoyed about the delay. Not only because we were anxious to tape some songs but because we felt we were being treated as people who didn't matter.

We taped several numbers and then returned to

Liverpool to wait. I returned to Decca again in March, on invitation for a lunch appointment. I felt pessimistic but tried not to show it when I met Beecher Stevens and Dick Rowe, two important executives. We had coffee, and Mr Rowe, a short plump man, said to me: 'Not to mince words, Mr Epstein, we don't like your boys' sound. Groups of guitarists are on the way out.'

I said – masking the cold disappointment which had spread over me: 'You must be out of your mind. These boys are going to explode. I am completely confident that one day they will be bigger than Elvis Presley.'

6

Yes!

'One day they will be greater than Presley.' Shadows of boredom flickered over the bland faces of the Decca executives. Hadn't every manager with something to sell offered them 'Britain's answer to Presley', or 'Decca's reply to Columbia's Cliff Richard'?

I have long since forgiven all the record companies their disbelief of my wilder claims. What I cannot understand or forget is their indifference to the *sound* of the Beatles on tape.

Mr Rowe and Mr Stevens pursued their point. 'The boys won't go, Mr Epstein. We know these things. You have a good record business in Liverpool. Stick to that.'

I was deeply disappointed but I was determined they wouldn't know, and as they piled pessimism on pessimism, I fought through the gloom to keep a calm front and I spoke quietly and at length about these Beatles who were the rage of Liverpool, who had ousted the Shadows as group heroes, four lads who played in a warehouse cellar by the Mersey.

The men of Decca took me to a luncheon in another room in the company headquarters. Whether it was the well-being of a good meal or my ceaseless talk of the Beatles' potential I don't know, but by the coffee stage there was a tiny crack in their determination not to record the boys.

I had paused in a long and probably overstated piece of sales-talk and the two men stared at each other. Dick Rowe drummed his fingers on the table and nodded knowingly. He turned to me and said: 'I have an idea that something might be done. You know who might help you? Tony Meehan.'

Meehan, one of the original Shadows, later to form a successful – though brief – partnership with Jet Harris, was then an A & R man with Decca and it was explained that I would be given the benefit of his experience and the use of a studio on payment of something approaching £100.

This annoyed me because I couldn't see why I should have to pay £100 to make one recording of a group who were going to conquer the entire record world. But it was stupid (I argued to myself in a frantic inward tussle between enthusiasm and anxiety about money) to turn down the first real concession I had won from Decca.

So, the following day I arrived at the Decca studios to meet Meehan. Dick Rowe was with him in the control room listening to a recording session and he nodded to me. After thirty minutes he introduced me to Meehan and said: 'Tony, take Mr Epstein out and explain the position.'

We left the room and went into another where there were two chairs facing each other. The A & R man, who two years later I was to book as a drummer on one of my Prince of Wales bills, looked me straight between the eyes without enthusiasm and said: 'Mr Epstein, Mr Rowe and I are very busy men. We know roughly what you require so will you fix a date for tapes to be made of these Beatles, phone my secretary and make sure that when you want the session, I am available?'

For the third time in three months I walked out of Decca with only the slightest whisper of hope. I was very upset and, I believed, almost at the end of my extended tether.

The date was arranged, but later abandoned because I felt that no useful purpose was served. I realised that there was nothing doing with Decca.

I hailed a taxi to Euston Station on the start of a glum cold journey to Lime Street Station where I telephoned Paul McCartney to ask the Beatles to meet me 'for a little talk'.

They arrived in the city centre and I took them to Joe's Cafe in Duke Street – a warm and friendly haunt of night-workers, drivers, young Beatles and anyone else with not a lot of money – anyone, in fact, who wants a cup of tea and a plate of chicken and chips and somewhere to go until 4 a.m.

We had a lot of tea and we smoked a little and I said this and that about the future and asked them about the beat scene in Liverpool. Then George, blowing a cloud of smoke in the air as if he couldn't care less about anything, suddenly turned to me and said: 'What about Decca, Brian?'

'I'm afraid it's no use,' I said. 'I've had a flat "No".'

None of the Beatles spoke. So I went on: 'And Pye have turned us down,' for I had also taken our beloved tapes to this other major company only to be rejected by their executives.

John picked up a teaspoon, flicked it high into the air and said: 'Right. Try Embassy.'

Embassy – the Woolworth's label where you can get low-priced copies of the pops on the counter next to the cold-cream and curling pins and the ice cream. This was not the grand breakthrough we had planned and dreamed about.

Embassy. John had broken the spell and the gloom vanished and we all talked at once about 'these rotten companies', and 'that lousy A & R man', and I decided with totally unjustifiable confidence that after a few days catching up on business affairs back in the Liverpool store, I would return to London with our tapes. Once again something in the Beatles was giving me strength and buoyancy.

On the local scene they were progressing well. The Beatles were booked on both sides of the Mersey, earning, when they played, £15 a night. I had finally secured their signatures on a contract on 24 January 1962, but, curiously, I had not, as I say, signed it myself. It provided them with safeguards against unemployment, protected them and me against any breach of faith and made the terms of my percentages quite clear.

Why had I not signed it? I believe it was because even though I knew I would keep the contract in every clause, I had not 100 per cent faith in myself to help the Beatles adequately. In other words, I wanted to free the Beatles of their obligations if I felt they would be better off.

I feel the same about them even now. I would not hold the Beatles or any artiste to contractual formalities if I learned that they didn't want to stay. There is no room in our relationships for contract-slavery.

In 1962, however, neither the Beatles nor I thought very much about our own contract. We were after the signature of a major recording executive on a stiff sheet of parchment. For the 1950s had made it clear that no artiste could succeed without records – and good records. The way to stardom lay in the charts.

During the lag between Decca's first session and the final refusal, we had played our first engagement as contracted artistes and manager at the Thistle Cafe, a genteel little spot on the seafront at West Kirby, an exclusive dormitory town on the estuary of the River Dee ten miles from Liverpool. Their success there, as at the Cavern, was an early sign that there was more than one-audience appeal in this group.

Our fee in West Kirby, by the way, was £18 out of which I took 36/- which just about covered petrol, oil, and wear and tear on tyres.

After the night in Joe's, I tackled a substantial backlog of work in Whitechapel, and told my father I wanted to take my tapes to London for an all-out, all-or-failure attack on the remaining record outlets. He agreed, provided it was only for a day or two, and I made, this time, for the HMV record centre in Oxford Street, London.

There I met Kenneth Boast, an exceedingly pleasant and interested executive with the HMV Retail Store within the mighty EMI company. Rather pompously, I told him I had tapes which were going to become very significant in British pop music, and he, being a nice chap, listened patiently to me, and to the tapes.

A technician making a record of my tapes – because I realised a record was handier to carry about and more convenient for people who might want to listen to Beatle music with a view to buying it – said to me: 'I don't think these are at all bad.' He told Boast who had a word with Syd Coleman, a music publisher, who had an office upstairs. Coleman became quite excited and said, 'I like these. I would be quite willing to publish them.'

So ignorant was I at that time that I thought this meant an immediate £50 on a publishing advance, because I really had no idea what publishing meant. Coleman also said he would speak to a friend of his at Parlophone, a man named George Martin. Said Coleman, 'I would like George to hear these. I think he might be very interested indeed.'

The acetones were made and Syd Coleman made his call. George Martin, an A & R man with Parlophone – a less fashionable label in those days – was away but Coleman arranged for me to meet George's delightful and gracious secretary and assistant, Judy Lockhart-Smith. She arranged for me to come to EMI the following day.

I was becoming very unpopular at home, for my father,

quite rightly, wanted to know whether I was employed by four leather-jacketed teenagers or by him. And if by him, when was I going to do some work?

Every day I spent in London increased his irritation. But I was adamant because I was determined not to give up the hunt for a record contract until I had been refused by every label in England. Even by Embassy.

So I allowed myself a final twenty-four hours to exhaust the remaining disc companies and I booked into the Green Park Hotel and tried, in vain, to sleep. I was worried about everything – the future of the Beatles who had shown such faith in my ability to make them stars, my own future with Nems, and the limits of my parents' patience.

In the morning I took a cab to the EMI offices in Manchester Square – part of a handsome building – to meet the man who would, within less than two years, produce sixteen number-one discs by my artistes.

George Martin was very helpful and discussed the difficulties of the record business, and the problems I would meet if I was going to be persistent, and said, 'I like your discs and I would like to see your artistes.' Wonderful news and we fixed a provisional date there and then. Martin I liked immensely. He is a painstaking man with a magnificent ear for music and a great sense of style. I do not think he could produce a bad disc.

Also at the offices I established an instant friendship with Judy Lockhart-Smith and there was an atmosphere about the place which gave me tremendous hope. George, a tall, thin elegant man with the air of a stern but fair-minded housemaster, had up to that time been doing good work with Peter Sellers on the famous and extremely successful LPs, but not very much with the new hard-driving beat music which was to sweep the world. He had a fine reputation, however, as a dedicated arranger, composer and oboist.

I liked the way he listened to the discs, his long legs crossed, leaning on his elbow; he rocked gently to and fro and nodded and smiled encouragingly. Judy also smiled her delicious smile and I sat with a face like stone as if my very life was at stake. In a way it was.

George had commented, 'I know very little about groups, Brian, but I believe you have something very good here,' and this to me had been the highest praise.

George also took the trouble to discuss the quality in this voice and that. He liked very much 'Hello Little Girl' recorded many months later and many hits later by the Fourmost – one of my Liverpool groups – but at that time it was merely one of many Beatle samples.

George also liked George Harrison on guitar and was excited about Paul's voice. 'He has the most commercial voice of the lot,' he commented and this is probably still true, though each Beatle has an equal amount to contribute to the total disc content.

We shook hands on the coming session, and though there was still no contract, I left EMI as the happiest Liverpudlian in London and I hurtled North with the wonderful news. I had phoned the Beatles to say I was arriving with news and when my train arrived at Lime Street the four of them were waiting on the platform – an unusual event for they are not sentimental people given to waving people off or to welcoming them back.

'Well,' said George. And eight eyes looked at me with scarcely suppressed excitement.

'You have a recording session at EMI as soon as you like,' I said and to celebrate we sped to the National Milk Bar in Liverpool where we got intoxicated with power and Coca-Cola and four packets of biscuits.

The Beatles were beside themselves with delight and relief. We planned a wild future of hit records and world tours and ticker-tape welcomes in every foreign capital. Kings, we dreamed, would want to meet us and dukes would seek autographs. Impossible fantasies were weaved until the milk bar closed. 'The evening's not going to stop now,' said John so we adjourned to a club and got pretty drunk and I lost a girlfriend called Rita Harris who worked for me and who said: 'I'm not going to compete with four kids who think they're entering the big time.'

Two years later the Beatles were the greatest entertainers in the world; they had met the Queen Mother and the Duke of Edinburgh and their pictures were on the walls of all the noble bedrooms of the young aristocracy. Prince Charles had all their records and San Francisco had the ticker-tape ready. They played the Hollywood Bowl, had the freedom of Liverpool. Ringo Starr was asked to be President of London University and John Lennon was the world's best-selling writer.

Back to June 1962 – the month of their first meeting with George Martin, and their introduction to Parlophone, whose profits they were to 'up' by some millions before they were through.

The early days ... a sprinkling of memories. Not all of them as happy as they seem.

Next page: Before ... the offer. Here was the raw material. Raw and rough but durable and very good. The Beatles in the leather-jacketed Hamburg days, 1961.

Left: The second of the great Liverpool groups signed by Epstein. The engaging hit-paraders, Gerry and the Pacemakers.

Below: The signing of Billy J. A key-day. It cost Epstein £50. Billy J. Kramer has since reaped thousands of pounds and won millions of fans.

The Boys
– with the
Master.

*Bottom
Right*:
Brian, with
tongue out,
announces
the name
'Beatles' at
a Liverpool
concert.
Paul
watches.

EMERGENCY EXIT

THIS DOOR IS AN
EMERGENCY EXIT ONLY
AND MUST BE KEPT CLOSED
Anyone using this EXIT
without authority will be
liable to instant dismissal

Preceding pages, left: Just for the camera. Brian and double bass. He plays not a note, neither reads nor writes music. But then ... neither do the Beatles.
Right: Early morning at Liverpool Docks and a few minutes of solitude.

The heart of the affair. Where the hits are born – the EMI recording studio in St John's Wood – home of 'She Loves You' and fifty more Lennon and McCartney recordings.

Overleaf: Reflections Parisian. Brian and the Beatles relaxing in the small hours at the King George V Hotel. They had just learned that their 'I Want to Hold Your Hand' was top of the US hit parade.

Left:
Brian and
car. A real
one and
costly.

Right:
Relaxing
with his
parents.

Overleaf:
Triumphal
return.
Down the
aircraft
steps after
their US
victories.

Miami, February 1964 – a few days away from the DJs and the turbulence of the heights of show business success.

Tycoonery. And the relentless symbol of
commercial pressures – the telephone.

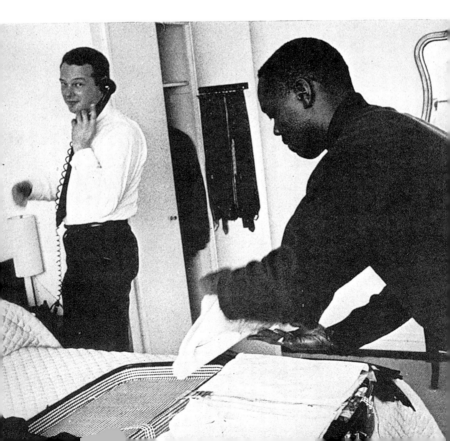

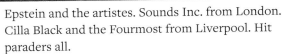

Epstein and the artistes. Sounds Inc. from London.
Cilla Black and the Fourmost from Liverpool. Hit
paraders all.

Overleaf, left: Brian in a mirror of his Knightsbridge flat. *Right:* Brian makes himself at home in a great London store.

Above: The pinnacle. Brian Epstein and the Beatles at their Royal Film Premiere with Princess Margaret.

Below: During the presentation of the Carl-Alan Awards the Duke of Edinburgh jokes with fellow-author John Lennon.

George liked them immensely and thought they were very polite and amusing. John Lennon was keen on George as a man to work with because he worshipped the Goons, and in particular, Sellers. George himself was anxious to make complete contact with these offbeat provincial lads and sought to establish it by asking: 'Let me know if there is anything you don't like.'

'Well, for a start,' said George Harrison, deadpan from under his fringe, 'I don't like your tie,' which Martin thought was as good a basis for friendship as anything. From that moment on they have been a dream of a team.

At the first EMI session the Beatles taped 'Love Me Do', a haunting piece by Paul and John which employed a harmonica, then a very original novelty which, like many Beatle innovations, has been overworked and debased since.

They also taped 'P.S. I Love You' and George Martin and his technicians liked them both. But there was still no contract and the Beatles and I left EMI full of hope but without money or security. They flew again to Hamburg for a further stint behind the vulgar neon of the Reeperbahn and I returned to Liverpool and the record store to wait for further news.

It came in July. I signed a recording contract with Parlophone Records. The Beatles were on the way and the £ sign which Parlophone use as a trademark was to become a symbol of unbelievable wealth.

I sent cables to all the boys in Germany. 'EMI contract signed, sealed. Tremendous importance to all of us. Wonderful.' They sent back postcards. From Paul: 'Please wire £10,000 advance royalties.' From John: 'When are we going to be millionaires.' 'Please order four new guitars' – from George.

They came back from Germany to a wild welcome in Liverpool, and on 11 September 1962, the Beatles made their first British disc ... 'Love Me Do' on the A-side, 'P.S. I Love You' on the B-side. It was released on 4 October and it came into the record charts forty-eight hours later at number 49. Finally it reached number 17 and the Beatles from Liverpool were in Britain's Top Twenty.

Their home city was thrilled beyond description. I had told everyone I knew that it was a magnificent disc, asked *Merseybeat* – the local music paper – to plug it and the kids of Liverpool bought it in thousands.

But there was a rumour – which lingered until it became acceptable currency – that I had bought the disc in bulk to get it into the charts. Possible though this would have been – had I the money, which I hadn't – I did no such thing, nor ever have. The Beatles, then as now, progressed and succeeded on natural impetus, without benefit of stunt or back-door tricks and I would like to make this quite clear.

'Love Me Do' was enough to convince all of us concerned with the Beatles – and by now I was no longer alone, since we had George Martin and a very nice and well-respected music publisher called Dick James on our side – that another disc must follow very quickly. Mitch Murray sent us a tune titled 'How Do You Do It?' which the Beatles attempted and didn't like. (It eventually went to a lad named Gerry Marsden ... but that is another story.) Paul and John submitted one of their own, appealingly called 'Please Please Me,' and it was made on 26 November 1962, and so pleased everyone that by early spring in 1963 it was clear leader of every disc chart in the country.

Inch by inch, the Beatles were creeping into the newspapers. Prophets, one knows, have a thin time in their own locality and though Tony Barrow – now one of my press officers, then a record reviewer – had been kind to 'Love Me Do', I had difficulty in 'selling' the importance of the Beatles to news editors and general-news columnists. I arranged a meeting with a writer on the *Liverpool Echo*, the namesake of Beatle George Harrison – though much older – and he met them for a drink in a Liverpool city-centre pub called The Dive.

But I don't think he liked them very much. He thought they lacked conventional manners and also they didn't buy drinks and they didn't make George Harrison's column 'Over the Mersey Wall' until he had a day off and another man, Bill Rogers, took it over. George Harrison was to become a friend and loyal supporter of the Beatles and a constant companion on our foreign trips.

Merseybeat, under the energetic editorship of Bill Harry, a self- taught expert on the beat scene, was pushing the Beatles very hard and I was grateful for this because I still had to make them a respected proposition for bookings in Northern halls. On one occasion I recall being paid in coins – £15 in sixpences and florins and even half-pennies – and I kicked up an awful fuss, not because £15 isn't £15 in any currency, but because I thought it was disrespectful to the Beatles. I felt that if one was to be a manager then one should fight for absolute courtesy towards one's artistes.

I didn't get the £15 in notes, by the way, but I had made my point and I and the Beatles felt better for it.

We entered 1963 full of confidence, our earnings up from that nightly £15 to £50; with new suits and one new Beatle. For Peter Best, drummer Beatle, had been replaced to his disappointment and to the dismay of many savage fans, by a little bearded chap from the Dingle ... His name was Richard Starkey but he called himself Ringo Starr.

7

Growth

In gold cowboy boots, with a grey streak in his hair and a desperado's thin moustache and beard, Ringo Starr was playing the drums at Butlin's holiday camp in Skegness in the summer of 1962 when the first crisis hit the Beatles under my management.

George Martin had not been too happy about Pete Best's drumming and the Beatles, both in Hamburg and at home, had decided his beat was wrong for their music. I wasn't sure about that and I was not anxious to change the membership of the Beatles at a time when they were developing as personalities. So I tried to talk to Pete about his drumming, without hurting his feelings, and at the same time I asked the Beatles to leave the group as it was.

They, however, had decided that sooner or later they wanted Pete to leave. They thought him too conventional to be a Beatle, and though he was friendly with John, he was not with George and Paul. And one night in September the three of them approached me and said: 'We want Pete out and Ringo in.'

I decided that if the group were to remain happy, Pete Best must go, and I knew that I would have to do it quickly and decisively. I had a sleepless night after mentioning casually to Pete that I would like him to call into the office the following day as there was something I wanted to discuss with him.

He arrived on time, as quiet as ever. I hedged a little and then said that we would be bringing in a new drummer for the Beatles, and I suggested many alternatives. That he could be the nucleus of a group which I would form, that he could be fitted into one of my existing groups and so on. None of these suggestions were acceptable and after two hours of talking around the subject Pete left the office very upset and pessimistic.

He failed to turn up that same day for an engagement at the River Park Ballroom in Chester and never again played with the Beatles.

Neil Aspinall, the faithful 'Nel', the Beatles' tough and brilliant road manager-guide-support, did however arrive, though he was a close friend of the Best family and he felt a great division in loyalty which he resolved in our favour. For this I am profoundly glad because I do not know how we should get the Beatles on the road without Nel. He is a splendid man, loved by all.

The sacking of Pete left me in an appalling position in Liverpool. Overnight I became the most disliked man on the seething beat scene. True, I had the support of the Beatles who were the city's darlings and they were delighted to have Ringo. But the fans wanted Pete Best as a Beatle and there were several unpleasant scenes.

For two nights I dared not go near the Cavern. Gangs prowled Mathew Street above the cellar club and chanting crowds cried: 'Pete for ever, Ringo never,' and waved banners. I could not stay away for too long so I applied to Ray McFall of the Cavern for a bodyguard and he sent along a massive doorman who hustled me and the Beatles as we ran a gauntlet of fists and jeers.

It was not a happy period, and though I dodged all the blows, George Harrison got a black eye which he took with him to the recording session as a proud symbol of his support of the new fourth Beatle.

Ringo settled in marvellously well and dissipated my early fears that he was not the right type. He shaved off his beard and combed his hair down and became pure Beatle. I remembered the phone conversation of initiation when John Lennon told him: 'You're in, Ringo. But the beard will have to go. You can keep your "sidies", though.'

Keep his 'sidies' he did and there isn't a better set of side whiskers in beat music, nor a more lovable man.

One problem of relationships remained as a result of Ringo's Beatledom, for he had been a valuable member of an excellent group called the Hurricanes, led by Rory Storme, one of the liveliest and most likeable young men on the scene. Rory was very annoyed when Ringo left and he complained to me. I apologised and Rory, with immense good humour, said: 'OK. Forget it. The best of luck to the lot of you.' I still see a fair amount of him for he is almost one of the fittings of Alan Williams's Blue

Angel club in Liverpool which is where beat groups go to relax.

Many other things had been happening in that first extraordinary year. I had become a full-blown manager of several first-class artistes.

After the Beatles I had signed Gerry and his Pacemakers, Billy J. Kramer and the Dakotas, and a group called the Big Three. I was taking a close interest in a slim, lively little thing called Priscilla White, and I had half an eye on the star potential of a freckled lad named Quigley. It was, in fact, all happening.

Gerry Marsden was one of the biggest stars in Liverpool, with a smile as wide as he was short, a huge generous personality and a fascinating voice, full of melody and feeling. With the Beatles he alternated at the most popular lunchtime sessions at the Cavern and I remember being amazed when I first spoke to him, early in 1962, to find that no one had ever approached him with a serious offer of management.

I felt that in him was much of the little folk-hero quality which had raised Tommy Steele to a position of importance in the theatre – the same native talent and warmth and instinctive showmanship. Events have proved me right and I am convinced that were it not for the Beatles, Gerry would have been Britain's number one young artiste.

I love watching Gerry at work – his communication with an audience, his winks and his nods and his feeling for humour or pathos. Offstage he is a robust and earthy character with an impressively salty vocabulary, but onstage he is the boy-next-door who would no more swear than miss an engagement. For this reason I protested once – and I rarely protest to newspapers – to a music paper who suggested I had ordered him to stop cursing during performances. The paper apologised the following week.

From the Cavern, Gerry moved swiftly through the ranks of groups to emerge as a huge crowd-puller on television, stage, in cabaret and, surely soon, in films. Princess Alexandra twice requested him for cabaret at society balls, and in the summer of this year the makers of *Tom Jones* produced him and the Pacemakers in his first feature-length film *Ferry Cross the Mersey*, for which he wrote all eight songs.

Gerry is no butterfly on the scene. He will be with us for a great many years because you cannot exhaust natural ability, and because a pop singer who sends his first three discs to the number-one spot in the disc charts does not do it by accident.

Away from his work, Gerry has been a wonderful friend to me. He is intelligent and kind, and more than any of the other artistes, he wants to demonstrate his friendship with presents. From him I've had gold cufflinks, bracelet, tie pins, and he remains the most outwardly grateful of all the people I have managed. Thankfully, one feels able to repay him with good work and a good future and I don't believe either I or George Martin or publisher Dick James ever had a fragmentary doubt about Gerry's worth as an entertainer.

Yet, in 1962, before what is now known as the Liverpool Sound was a passport to success, even Gerry had to be sold hard to the commercial interests who make up the entertainment industry. George Martin himself had to be convinced and for this purpose I persuaded him to come north with Judy to see Gerry at work.

Gerry had been a little impatient for a disc for, though I had signed him in June, there was still no sign of a recording contract in December. I had stalled because I wanted 'Love Me Do' and the Beatles to get away, but as Christmas approached, I realised that Gerry needed some tangible proof that he was important to me. I asked George to come to Merseyside. On 12 December he suddenly decided to come and I was in a frightful panic, for this was one of the few days on which Gerry had no booking. At the last moment I managed to fix a junior date – for under fifteens – at the Majestic Ballroom in Birkenhead. It would have been awful for George to arrive to see my new star and find him without work.

Gerry was splendid with the kids and George was very impressed – particularly with Gerry singing the new number 'How Do You Do It?' which, three months later, was to win him a silver disc. But contrary to a half-true press story which, I'm ashamed to say, we put out without George's knowledge, Gerry was not signed on the spot. George simply said: 'Come to London and we'll give you a test.'

At any rate, Gerry went to London and has since sold many more than a million discs.

Later that night George, Judy and I went to the Cavern where the Beatles were playing. They had become very 'hot' in Liverpool not only because they were the best group in the city but because they had become a sensation with a record actually in the national charts. The four of them – John, Paul, George and Ringo – were now a well-knit unit with Pete Best a figure in the past, and they looked pretty splendid, wearing black velvet waistcoats and trousers, white shirts and black silk knitted ties.

George was thrilled with the Cavern and planned to make an LP, live in the cellar. It hasn't happened yet but there is still time.

It was very warm in the Cavern that night, though outside a wild December gale was blowing over the Mersey, and we left our coats with a chirpy cloakroom attendant with bright orange hair. George, who responds quickly to a feminine smile, was impressed enough to murmur to me: 'Pretty girl, Brian,' and I agreed. Her name was Priscilla and given second sight, we would all have been interested to know that eighteen months later that lively cloakroom girl was to emerge as Britain's leading girl singer with a season at the London Palladium and two magnificent discs far and away at the head of the record charts – 'Anyone Who Had a Heart' and 'You're My World'.

The girl, of course, was Cilla Black, then named Priscilla White. My lovely Cilla – one of the very great stars of the future – the most photographed girl in England, the singer everyone loves and admires but whom no one envies because of her utter simplicity.

Cilla was one of the girls who was always around the Cavern. She was a singer, I knew, but I had no idea that she took music seriously – practically everyone in and around the Cavern was some sort of singer or guitarist

– and though I liked Cilla I had no ideas of management until midway through 1963.

I first heard her sing with the Beatles in Birkenhead but had not been greatly impressed because the acoustics had been wrong for her voice, but the next occasion was early one morning in the Blue Angel Club in Liverpool. She looked, as always, magnificent – a slender graceful creature with the ability to shed her mood of dignified repose if she were singing a fast number. I watched her move and I watched her stand and I half closed my eyes and imagined her on a vast stage with the right lighting. I was convinced she could become a wonderful artiste.

Cilla was that morning singing with a jazz group, but she had also done a few numbers – for nothing – with the Beatles and with other Liverpool groups including, notably, King Size Taylor and the Dominoes. I went across to her after her last number and I said: 'I thought that was absolutely wonderful. Have you ever thought of turning professional?' She laughed that wild joyous laugh which later won her millions of fans on *Juke Box Jury*, and said: 'Who'd have me?'

I said: 'Me, for one. Would you care to have a manager? I can't promise anything yet but I think you would be a very good recording artiste.' Cilla said, 'Hmmm. Well, it's a bit risky, but I love singing, and if I could make a success of it, it'd be great.'

So a few days later I made a firm offer of management and asked Cilla to take a long time to think it over. She did and she signed a contract with me in September 1963. Eight months later she had become the girl-symbol of

British youth, the most exciting singer in Britain and a limitless source of pride to me.

Cilla has never given me a moment's anxiety. Her style and her natural ease make her a joy to manage but, curiously, she was innocently involved in one of the most frightening experiences of my life.

News that I was soon to sign a management agreement with her had spread swiftly around Liverpool and in the small hours one morning I had an anonymous telephone call. On the other end of the line there was a thick, coarse voice which said, baldly: 'Keep off Cilla White, Epstein. She doesn't need your management. She's signed with friends of mine.'

The caller then hung up, leaving me wondering why I should buy myself a problem like this. The following morning, I realised that this was precisely what the caller had wanted – to scare me off.

I spoke to Cilla and she assured me she had no agreement with anyone else and I decided to take no more notice of the call. But at about 2 a.m. another call came. It was a different voice but the message was much the same. This time I was able to speak and I said: 'Neither Miss White nor I are the least bit interested in this nonsense,' and this time I hung up. The calls persisted for a few days but the claims and threats became more and more feeble until they finally stopped. I was very relieved because I didn't wish – and never will want – to pirate artistes.

Cilla was the last Liverpool artiste I secured and she is, of course, the only girl. This is not accidental; for I was finding it difficult, in the first case, to select talent from so much in the beat city, and, in the second case, I didn't care to dilute the special attention I wanted to give Cilla by managing a girl-competitor. The disc charts cannot stand very many girls, however gorgeous they may look onstage.

After the Beatles and Gerry, with great care and precision, I selected four more Northern groups to present Tin Pan Alley with an irresistible onslaught. I signed Billy J. Kramer from Liverpool and linked him with Manchester's four-man Dakota group, not only because I like the Dakotas' work, but also because Billy's own group, the Coasters – now with Chick Graham – did not wish to turn professional.

Billy Kramer had in fact won a prize as a result of a poll organised by *Merseybeat* for the best-known non-professional group in Liverpool. Nems gave the prize and it was partly because I was impressed with this achievement that I signed him, and also because John Lennon of the Beatles thought a lot of Kramer's voice. He was, I thought, an outstanding artiste for his age and experience.

Also from the Cavern Scene I took on the Big Three – a group which has changed membership to such an extent that half Liverpool seems to have played with them at one time or another – the Fourmost and the Remo Four.

The Big Three are no longer with me. I gave up management because the group broke and I don't approve of groups breaking, particularly as, in this case, the mainstay of the group left and the balance was lost.

Balance, in groups as in life, is all.

This group, when I took them on, had a very good sound and I was most optimistic, but there was a lack of discipline and this cannot be tolerated because it is bad for business, awful for reputation and extremely bad for morale.

I was sorry to lose them because Johnny Hutchinson, one of the original members, was a good drummer. And vocalist Johnny Gustafson, bass guitarist – now with the Merseybeats – is a very fine property, strong musically and physically and very good-looking.

With the Fourmost – in contrast – I have had an increasingly happy relationship and they are now one of the country's leading groups, full of fun and brain, with a lot of the reckless charm of the Beatles. They, more than any of the others, were the most difficult to secure for a contract, for though they were old hands at the Cavern and enjoyed playing, they were firmly involved in apprenticeships or at college and they didn't wish to know about management or full-time professionalism.

Between them they have twenty-seven GCE passes – I remember being impressed by this since I had none – and they had promising careers ahead of them. But I felt sure I could offer them a solid living in music and so it has turned out. It was George Martin who convinced me they were ripe for development for he heard them at the Cavern and said: 'I would like to meet them sometime and see if we can't make a hit or two.'

So be it. He met them, I signed them and a hit or two or three they have made. They opened at the London Palladium with Cilla in May and of them the theatre critic of *The Times* said in his notice: 'For sheer charm they stole the show.'

Billy J. Kramer, perhaps in some ways the best-looking pop singer in the world, if I may lapse into superlative, sent his first two songs to the number-one spot and that's not a bad start. He was another of the Cavern crowd – a tall, well-made ex-railway lad christened William Ashton. Paul and John wrote his first three numbers: 'Do You Want to Know a Secret', 'Bad to Me' and 'I'll Keep you Satisfied'.

Inexplicably – though you can't win them all – the third failed to make number one but Billy and the Dakotas compensated by crashing to the top with 'Little Children' in England and near the top in America.

His success in the States was particularly pleasing for it consolidated my success over there and proved to me that it was not only Beatlemania that impressed the Americans.

My first solo artiste was a freckled-faced boy called Quigley and his discovery was more like the American film/musical conception of star-making than any of the other people I manage. It happened one night in a hall in Widnes in 1962. I was running Monday night concerts there, with Gerry and the Beatles and other fairly well-established performers, and the eight to eight-thirty spot was occupied by 'unknowns' who used the opportunity for a form of audition. I paid them nothing but they got themselves a hearing.

One night I was in the manager's office – discussing takings, no doubt, for though I love not money, I adore takings – when I heard a very fascinating voice over the amplification system. I ran from the office into the hall and saw a youth in a depressing green suit, singing his heart out to the great delight of a young, mostly female, audience. I thought he was excellent – with a lot of mischief in his presence and much voice in his lungs.

When he came offstage I spoke to him and he said his name was Tom Quigley. 'No,' he said he was not managed, but he wouldn't mind. I said I couldn't offer him management but I would like to assist him in his career, and much later Bob Wooler of the Cavern came and told me that Quigley was a little unhappy. He had no job and he was receiving offers of management, was I prepared to take him on full-time? So I did and the relationship has worked, very well. He has changed his name to Quickly and he is going to be a star.

8

Beatlemania

Beatlemania descended on the British Isles in October 1963. It happened suddenly and dramatically and we weren't prepared for it.

The Beatles say it started when they returned from Sweden after a five-day working trip. I believe it started earlier when they were named for the *Royal Variety Show* at the Prince of Wales Theatre in London. At this time, although it is less than a year ago, the Beatles were still performing in ballrooms for comparatively small fees, and it was possible to see them and visit their shows without fighting through a crowd of screaming teenagers – until the *Royal Show*.

When this news broke – and I felt it was inevitable that the show-business sensation of 1963 should be represented in this show – pressmen from Liverpool poured into a Southport ballroom to see the Beatles. The boys themselves were alarmed. They were accustomed to press interest but not to a solid wall of implacable questioning, which is what they faced that night.

The general trend of the questions was: 'Why not?' And Ringo said: 'I want to play the drums before the Queen Mother. Is there anything wrong in that?' The press agreed that there was not but this first hint of widespread interest – outside teenage record bars – was to me a significant change in attitude.

For the first time the Beatles were being challenged about their loyalty to the very young – and about their recognition of their lowly beginnings.

Well, they played the *Royal Show* and London was brought to a standstill by the screaming youth of the South of England. The Royal Family, the wealthy and the great were captivated by the naturalness of the four young men and we were all very proud.

On the show with them was Marlene Dietrich, who was herself won over by the backstage aplomb of entertainers young enough to be her grandchildren. She said to me later: 'It was a joy to be with them. I adore these Beatles.'

The Beatle Queue became a feature of British life. With transistors and blankets, hot-water bottles, and with or without their parents' blessing, the young people of provincial England braved every weather hazard for a small slip of paper which would permit them, for twenty-five minutes, to view and hear their idols.

Hundreds of thousands were disappointed, for several teenagers – and spivs, or teenagers hired by spivs – were buying them up en bloc. But this didn't seem to matter. It was enough to have been involved in Beatlemania. The press, slow at first, decided to take an active part in their promotion of Beatle-interest without, I should say, any prompting from me, for it was in October that I had the first warning of the dangers of over-exposure.

Daily, articles appeared on the front pages of the great national newspapers.

The *Daily Telegraph*, 28 October, quoted: '... Police at Newcastle upon Tyne struggled yesterday with screaming teenagers fighting to get tickets for the Beatles "pop" group. A policewoman was kicked ...'

(Note that even as recently as October it was necessary to elaborate and say Beatles 'pop' group.)

In Newcastle – and this was typical – nearly four thousand Beatle fans had queued in freezing conditions for tickets. Said the *Telegraph*: 'It looked more like a death watch than the prelude of a joyous Beatle event.... Three ambulances, rarely short of patients, some of them school girls, dealt with more than a hundred cases of fainting or exhaustion. Several were treated at hospital. Seventy-four police were on duty and special check points had to be set up.'

At Hull there were still three thousand in a Beatle queue after five thousand tickets had been sold. A senior police officer told the *Daily Telegraph*: 'This has been an incredible night,' and at Coventry a theatre manager said: 'I have never known anything like it. The queues and the excitement are beyond belief.'

It was the same throughout Britain. The Beatles had ceased to be purely a pop group and were becoming a cult. The concerts themselves were wild and exciting, and successful to an extent I had never thought possible.

Every ticket could have been sold twice over, and after the early scenes of the ticket queues the concerts themselves consolidated the view of everyone in show business that the Beatles were the biggest thing since Sinatra in the 1940s. All of us involved with them – everyone who had known them at the Cavern – were serenely proud.

When, on 31 October, the Beatles arrived home from Sweden they could not believe what they heard. Thousands of howling, screaming fans had converged on London Airport hours before their plane was due in, and crush barriers had been erected to keep the youngsters from the tarmac. Paul said later: 'It has all been happening in England while we were away. We were amazed because although we had had several number ones in the record charts, teenage interest had only been on the normal, pop level.'

There were questions in Parliament about the queues and about the safety of teenagers outside theatres. 'Shouldn't we,' suggested one MP, 'withdraw the police and see what happens?' and George told a reporter: 'If they do, the injuries would be their own fault. We don't want people to get hurt.'

Curiously, though mob-attention had never been more dramatic or extensive, there was no violence. I am not being priggish when I say that the Beatles have never been associated with actual rioting, vandalism or damage of any sort, I don't know why this is so, but it is. The 1955 wave of hooliganism in the days of Bill Haley and 'Rock Around the Clock' was quite another matter. Seats were slashed, cinemas burned, windows broken, and policemen and passers-by attacked.

Yet, though the Beatles' music is rock and roll, though it is as exciting and stimulating as the mid-fifties version, it has remained remote from savagery. And even this year, no one – not even the most resentful – levelled any charges at the Beatles when the Mods and the Rockers battled it out on the beaches of south-east England.

Far from the key cinemas and the beat centres of Britain, the Beatles were becoming a household word. Naturally, I found it impossible to enter a discussion without the Beatles being mentioned. But men, women and children of all ages, all classes, all shades of belief and intelligence were finding the same problem.

The Beatles undoubtedly became the chief talking point of 1963. A journalist told me in October: 'By Christmas it will be impossible to look at the front page of any newspaper in England without seeing a reference to them,' and he was right.

We became, all of us, over-exposed. At first the sight of the Beatles in the newspapers, the discussion of their views, their habits, their clothes, was exciting. They liked it and so did I because it was good for them and it was good for business.

But finally it became a great anxiety. How much longer, I wondered, could they maintain public interest without rationing either their personal appearances or their newspaper coverage? In fact, by a stringent watch on their contacts with the press and a careful and constant check on their bookings, we just averted saturation point. But it was very close, and other artistes have been destroyed by this very thing.

By 1964 it had become fashionable to be a Beatle fan. There were no longer any barriers of any sort. Grandmothers and tiny children joined the middle- and teen-age ranks and, as a result, we could expect a certain million sale in England alone of any new release. By the summer of this year, practically every senior citizen, king of commerce, aristocrat or charity organiser was clamouring to illuminate his name or his industry or his promotion with the name 'Beatle'. It became clear that if you had a Beatle at a party you were 'made' socially.

In my brief lifetime I have never known anything like it. The boys themselves took it very blandly because it was, after all, only two years since they had fought to increase their earnings from 25/- a night to £3/10/-.

But apart from Stockholm, there was little interest overseas at this stage. The huge key American market had yet to be conquered, and far away in Australia no one was the least bit bothered.

In January this year, when the Beatles went to Paris, there were forty curious pressmen at Le Bourget Airport, but no fans. Not all the tickets at the Olympia Theatre had been sold. But by the end of three weeks there were wailing, chanting mobs surging around the theatre, and baton-charging gendarmes were on nightly patrol in their hundreds.

Paris stores were full of Beatle wigs and several of them relayed the songs of Paul and John eight hours daily over their loudspeaker systems.

Paris fell – later, dramatically, America of course and,

in the summer, Copenhagen, Amsterdam and the whole of Australasia followed.

Every crowd record in every country they visited was broken. In Amsterdam, 150,000 of the townspeople packed the banks and the bridges of the canals to watch the four young men take a ninety-minute boat tour. Again, all ages, all classes and both sexes.

Even in Hong Kong, the placid, phlegmatic Chinese were overwhelmed by the curious alchemy and the pounding beat of the mop-heads as the Americans had christened them. Police in all these centres admitted that the experience was new and overwhelming.

When the Beatles arrived in Adelaide in June this year, it was in response to a petition signed by 80,000 townspeople. Nearly a third of a million citizens lined the Anzac Highway from the airport to the city centre, cheering and applauding, waving flags, throwing streamers, garlands and flowers in the path of the Beatles' open car as if it were a Caesar returning from the wars.

Happy and gay though they are, teenagers milling in their thousands around town halls and hotels and theatres would kill the Beatles if they got their hands on them.

Fans unleashed on one of their idols would be murderous. This is why the apparent imprisonment of the Beatles is essential.

One of the facts of life which they and those around them have to learn is that freedom of movement is no longer possible. I had my first taste of crowd mania on a railway station in Washington, when a solid wall of clambering ecstatic teenagers drove me to the edge of the platform as an express train thundered in from New York.

It was snowing and I slithered on my knees and was only saved when a security man – himself hanging from another man's belt – grabbed my ankle and hauled me into the comparative safety of the mob.

It is sad that the fans cannot see more of the Beatles and vice versa. We feel it especially outside theatres and in hotel lobbies when they wait for hours to catch a glimpse of a head or a smile. But it is at these very points that we must exercise the greatest caution.

The getaway car is our lifeline to work and freedom. This, normally, is an Austin Princess which can comfortably seat four Beatles, their road manager and, if necessary, a security officer or policeman.

In England the driver is always the same, a huge man called Bill Corbett, who knows the problems, chief of which is the ability to speed fast enough to frighten fans out of the way, but not so fast that they get run over.

It is commonplace for fans to hurl themselves at a Beatle vehicle if it is travelling at anything less than twenty miles an hour.

After a concert in London one night four of John's admirers wrenched off a near-side door and hurled themselves into the vehicle. The fans were fought out and Corbett drove off without the door, with the four Beatles huddled against the wind.

He returned later for the door, to find that it had been captured as a souvenir.

Every entry and exit to the theatre is carefully planned

between road manager, driver, police and theatre manager. There are various systems to avoid trouble. One is to use rear and side entries – the obvious one. Another – the least apparent – is to swing the car to the front entrance to allow the boys to dash through the main foyer.

A third system involves the use of decoy cars or armoured police vans which draw the fans to one side of the theatre while the Beatles slide quietly in the other side.

Very often – for getting out of the theatre – the Beatles and I have been taken in tunnels beneath the theatre into the adjoining building to be released more than a hundred yards away from the outer circle of fans. Rather like POW escapes.

It is all very exciting the first few times. For the Beatles it is a routine part of life.

Abroad, we are often at the mercy of inefficient or over-zealous police forces. The chief feature of all things Beatle is that they are unprecedented. Police who believe they know all about crowds and fans admit, after a Beatle visit, that they had never known anything like it.

Frequently, for instance, the police undervalue the magnetism of McCartney or underestimate the determination of girls to tear at his clothes.

In Holland, however, the police took no chances and punched, swung and hurled my assistant, Derek Taylor, and road manager, Neil Aspinall, to the ground half a dozen times a day because they thought they were trying to attack the Beatles.

The Dutch police, in their enthusiasm to protect the

four long-haired young men, did everything on a majestic scale. Even on a run to the country, masses of jack-booted, helmet-clad officers on motorcycles and sidecars flanked the Beatles' car, telephoning constantly to a central control point while, at front and rear, police cars with sirens and blue lights shrieked and flashed warnings.

It would probably have been much more effective to drive them quietly in one private car – though not nearly so exhilarating.

On the first American trip squads of private detectives were engaged to protect the Beatles' hotel suite, to guard them while relaxing. But, even so, two girls almost succeeded in being delivered as a parcel to the Beatles' room.

It was, incidentally, in Miami that my then press officer, Brian Sommerville, remarked to the Chief of Police: 'I am told that in Miami you have the best police money can buy ...' A statement memorable for the innocence of its ambiguity.

Arrangements in Australia, though smooth, were different. We worked not on a dramatic flashing-light, strong-arm system, but with two small cars, which would have been quite anonymous but for the posters and the letters on the side proclaiming the Beatles.

We relied on the restraint of crowds, and largely they were very well behaved, barring the near-destruction of Ringo Starr when he arrived at the Southern Cross Hotel. Had the police not rescued him, the Beatles would still have been without their regular drummer – possibly for ever.

Australian crowds were unquestionably the largest we had ever known, certainly the friendliest. But still we dare not underestimate the violent potential of 20,000 surging human beings. Indoors, one often feels less safe than in the street.

At an elegant civic reception in Adelaide, autograph pencils flashed like knives around the valuable features of Lennon, Harrison and McCartney, and it was a relief when the Lord Mayor of Melbourne barred autographs at his reception in honour of the Beatles. There, too, there was one tricky incident when a young man made an offensive remark about the length of Ringo's hair, repeated it and then lunged forward to grab it.

He was jabbed smartly in the ribs by the sharp elbow of an otherwise non-violent Beatle-minder and later complained, with surprising naïvety, that he had been attacked.

Ringo's hair is an occupational hazard. For at the sprawling, appalling British Embassy reception in Washington there was the incident of the scissors when a guest snipped off a curl of the famous locks.

Is it surprising that we take a long hard look at receptions at embassies?

The Beatles run other risks – the more obvious ones are onstage in the worldwide barrage of jelly beans, pennies, toys, autograph books and, indeed, anything throwable.

Paul was nearly blinded once by a safety pin; George took a sharp knock in Hong Kong when a silver dollar struck him on the ear. Thus are the many demonstrations of love manifested violently.

End-of-show enthusiasm can sometimes be alarming. Excited fans can leap to the stage in a second or two, and Billy J. Kramer recently fled for his life at an aristocratic gathering in England when a number of our future leaders stormed him and the group. He escaped unhurt, but several fans were trampled and his equipment was wrecked.

It is not all danger, however, and I find all large gatherings of fans immensely exhilarating and thrilling. I can think of no warmer experience than to be in a vast audience at a Beatle concert.

I hope Beatle crowds continue to scream themselves hoarse in a frenzy of exultation.

I hope everybody has a wildly, wonderfully good time. For this – and only this – is what the Beatles are all about.

9

Them

John ... Paul ... George. And Ringo. Collectively the four most famous names in the world. Extraordinary young men who have directly altered the lives of hundreds, even thousands of people, who have affected the entire balance of the entertainment industry, who have kicked up so much dust that in all our lifetimes it will not completely settle.

They are daily conversation in hundreds of millions of homes throughout the world. More has been written about them than about any other entertainer of any era. The haunted, wonderful wistful eyes of little Ringo Starr from Liverpool's Dingle are more instantly recognisable than any single feature of any of the world's great statesmen.

The superlatives of the industry in which they belong, though gross and wild and overstated, cannot begin to describe the impact of four young men in their early twenties, who left school before they should, who can neither read music nor write it, who care not a fig or a damn or a button for anyone save a tight, close-guarded clique of less than a dozen.

For John, Paul, George and Ringo are themselves the ultimate superlative. They have defied analysis, though not for a year or two has there been a shortage of analysists prepared to devote an amazing amount of time to delving, scratching and soul-baring to look for a reason for the inhuman grip of the Beatles.

I have known them so long, so well and with such personal involvement that I rarely try to examine what has happened or why. I was there when the foursome was born – when the face of Ringo slotted into the curious chemical pattern and thus created the four-constituent formula which has driven the young womanhood of the world into a demented frenzy of exultation and admiration.

Yet I cannot pretend that, facially, Ringo seemed to me to be the perfect fit. And certainly the other three did not band together originally because they knew that somehow they were to become a hypnotic blend. George and Paul and John linked up simply because they were three teenagers keen on making music and because they could do it without rowing or arguing over small things.

In other words they got on well together, and when the disappearance of Pete Best left them without a drummer, they asked for Ringo because he could do the job and because they liked him.

But ... But it is inescapable that Ringo was the catalyst for the others. He certainly completed the jigsaw and the Beatles with Ringo became a magnet for the great camera-artists of the world, a target for the jaded, lately hostile eyes of people who had hardly known that popular music existed.

I am not here discussing their music at all, though, of course, it was and is this which is the core and reality of their success and the Beatles themselves would not give a fragment of a moment's thought to anything as abstruse as chemical appeal or collective magnetism. But I believe that there is something a little outside our normal experience in the Happening of the Beatles and I believe it is valuable to make the point. It may be magic or it may be some strange organic combination. Whatever it is, it is there and it goes far beyond 'Twist and Shout' or 'She Loves You'.

There was, of course, another famous foursome – though in fiction – and, strangely, they started as a threesome and only realised complete fulfilment when the fourth was added. They were Athos, Porthos, Aramis – and D'Artagnan. They were slightly outside society, yet socially acceptable, nonconformist but in no way outlawed.

This, in essence, is the Beatles. They are British, but un-English in that they accept barriers neither of class nor sex. And for this all classes and both sexes adore them. They are of Liverpool with its hard, flat humour, but they have a far wider, more way-out private world of inward smiles than the average earthy Liverpudlian. They are pop stars with little respect for the specious values of the industry.

The Beatles don't say 'Glad to meet you', but they often

are. They don't flatter women but they never sit while a woman stands. They have their own rules and one may not understand them but they are workable, and they have never damaged anyone outside which is more than one can say for some of Society's rules.

I am always being asked: 'What are the Beatles *really* like?' I never know quite what to say because they are what they are and anyone who has ever seen or heard them either in person or on radio or screen has, basically, as much chance as I have of knowing what they are like. I believe, and I must say it, that they are quite magnificent human beings, utterly honest, often irritating but splendid citizens shining in a fairly ordinary, not very pleasing world.

In many ways they are the same now as they were when I first met them. Immeasurably richer of course, with a rounder confidence and a rational consciousness of their status in the hierarchy of popular music, but they have not become arrogant and they never will.

Much nonsense has been written of the Liverpool Sound, as if it were some instantly recognisable package deal in electronic music. Of course, it is no such thing. There is, for instance, no common sound linking the Beatles with the Searchers, or Billy J. Kramer with the Fourmost. And Gerry and the Pacemakers are like none of these.

What there is between all these groups is their origin as Liverpudlians and it is this basic take-everything-in-your-stride provincialism, born of life in a raw seaport on the edge of England, which sustains them in the face of their incalculable fame and international adulation. At the centre of the storm which has surrounded them for nearly two years the Beatles are very calm. They have somehow found a little island where the gale of press and public becomes a mild and gentle breeze which leaves them rich and contented but undamaged.

I have no favourites among the Beatles and this they realise now but it wasn't always so. A manager dealing with a close-knit foursome has to be as fair as and as cautious as a father of four children. And one night very early in my management of the Beatles this was brought home to me with an unpleasant thump.

In the long-ago days of 1962 the Beatles had a van for their equipment which on occasions was also used to transport them. But whenever I could I would drive to each of the Beatles' homes and collect them for a show. This particular night I called on John first then on George and then on Paul – Peter Best was travelling in the van.

George got out of the car and knocked on Paul's door in the little street where he lived in Allerton. He knocked for a few moments and there was still no sign of Paul. Finally Paul answered and said, 'Tell Brian I'm not ready and I'll be a while.' George came back to the car and told me this. I said: 'Well, he should be ready. I said I'd be here at eight and it's past eight.' George went back to the house, returned a minute later and said Paul still was not ready. I said: 'George, tell him we're going to the Beehive for a drink and if he likes he can get the bus to the city centre, the train to Birkenhead and another bus to the Technical College.'

It was a very important evening because we were making money at last and the Technical College show was a good one, in a good hall, and was completing an otherwise successful three-part engagement for Liverpool University. Also we had another concert much later that night at New Brighton Tower. We went to the Beehive pub and from there one of the Beatles telephoned Paul. I believe it was John. He came back from the phone and said: 'Paul now says he's not coming. He's very annoyed at having to get the train and the bus.'

I was worried, angry and upset, and I toyed with the idea of telling Paul that I would not be bothered with managing the Beatles if this was the way they were going to behave.

I went into the Nems office to telephone Paul and the other Beatles went home. I spoke to his father – a very charming and gentle person – who said Paul was upset and would not be able to attend the shows. Paul, however, relented much later, we gathered the other Beatles and we rushed to New Brighton Tower where we were able to catch up and give the university concert.

This was the only time any one of the Beatles refused to play and it could never happen now. But it was not the only time one or more of the Beatles fell out with me. It would not be normal or reasonable to expect four artistic men to glide through life without a clash of views, and although rows are rare, they happen.

Paul can be temperamental and moody and difficult to deal with but I know him very well and he me. This means that we compromise on our clash of personalities. He is

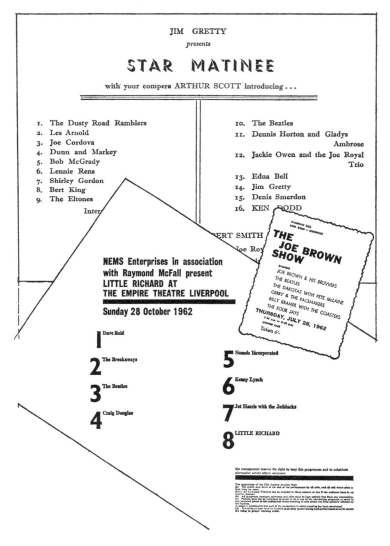

In the beginning ... some early Beatles programmes.

a great one for not wishing to hear about things, and if he doesn't want to know he switches himself off, settles down in a chair, puts one booted foot across his knee and pretends to read a newspaper, having consciously made his face an impassive mask.

But he has enormous talent and inside he has a great tenderness and great feeling which are sometimes concealed by an angry exterior. I believe that he is the most obviously charming Beatle with strangers, autograph hunters, fans and other artistes. He has a magnificent smile and an eagerness both of which he uses, not for effect, but because he knows they are assets which will bring happiness to those around him.

Paul is very much a world star, very musical, with a voice more melodic than John's and therefore more commercially acceptable. Also, and this is vital to me, he has great loyalty to the other Beatles and to the organisation around him. Therefore, I ignore his moods and hold him in high esteem.

I would not care to lose him as a friend.

John Lennon, his friend from boyhood, his co-writer of so many songs, the dominant figure in a group which is, virtually, without a leader, is, in my opinion, a most exceptional man. Had there been no Beatles and no Epstein participation, John would have emerged from the mass of the population as a man to reckon with. He may not have been a singer or a guitarist, a writer or a painter, but he would most certainly have been a Something. You cannot contain a talent like this. There is in the set of his head a controlled aggression which demands respect.

David Ash, a feature-writer on the *Daily Express* once described this face: '... it has the fear-neither-God-nor-man quality of a Renaissance painter's aristocrat ...'

Beautifully put and I don't think this will be bettered, though, like the other Beatles, John would regard this sort of description as soft, stupid. They are wary of overstatements, chiefly because they are surrounded and swamped by it, not only from fans but the from essential hard-sell vocabulary of the show-business world.

Who writes the words and who the music? So people ask endlessly. The answer is that both write both and that sometimes John will do a song completely by himself, words and music, and that sometimes Paul will arrive with a completed number. But neat and tidy and honest though John's lyrics are, they represent only a fraction of his real aptitude for words.

For John, the pop singer from Liverpool, was guest of honour at a Foyle's lunch to mark the success of his splendid book, *John Lennon in his own Write*, an extraordinary collection of verse, prose and drawings, done by him off-the-cuff, without training or guidance. It sold more than 100,000 copies in Britain, topped the best-seller list and was marvellously well reviewed.

I was not the least bit surprised but I was deeply gratified that a Beatle could detach himself completely from Beatleism and create such impact as an author.

And made no speech.

In answer to the toast he stood, held the microphone, and said: 'Thank you all very much. You've got a lucky face.' Sir Alan Herbert, who was sitting beside me, said later: 'A shameful affair, he should most certainly have made a speech.'

But here John was behaving like a Beatle. He was not prepared to do something which was not only unnatural to him, but also something he might have done badly. He was not going to fail. After the luncheon he commented: 'Give me another fifteen years, I might make a speech. Not yet.' And I agreed with him. I rely on John's instinct and, in fact, on the instinct of all the Beatles, not only on music, but in matters of taste and style and general behaviour.

I believe I always knew that I was dealing with people who were not just a pop group, but were exceptional human beings. John's wit and flair were apparent when I first met him and his old-young bearing was obviously right for public appearances.

None of the Beatles suffer fools gladly. John suffers them not at all and can be very acid, even cruel, if he is goaded. A silly woman approached him in Paris, peered into his face and said: 'It isn't! It is. Is it? It's you. A real live Beatle!'

John stared at her, his lids hooding his eyes, 'What sort of an approach is this?' he asked and he did a wild, terrifying dervish dance around her. Frightened out of her life, the lady fled down the corridor of the George V Hotel and never again I suspect will she peer into the face of a Beatle, as if she is in a zoo.

At the Foyle's lunch, when John was besieged by a great many fighting middle-aged ladies who should have known better, one woman clutching ten copies of his book for autograph, said: 'Put your name clearly just here,' and she prodded a page with a grossly over-jewelled finger. John looked at her, astonished, and she turned to a friend jammed against her and said: 'I never thought I would stoop to asking for such an autograph.' 'And I never thought,' remarked John, 'that I would be forced to sign my name for someone like you.'

Sometimes he has been abominably rude to me. I remember once attending a recording session at EMI studios in St John's Wood. The Beatles were on the studio floor and I was with their recording manager George Martin in the control room. The intercom was on and I remarked that there was some sort of flaw in Paul's voice in the number 'Till There Was You'.

John heard it and bellowed back: 'We'll make the record. You just go on counting your percentages.' And he meant it. I was terribly annoyed and hurt because it was in front of all the recording staff and the rest of the Beatles. We all looked at one another and felt uncomfortable and John turned away, indicating that there was no apology coming. I left the studios in a sort of sullen rage.

Later we had it out, but he told me quite emphatically that it was not cruelly intended and only meant in fun. He is a full and generous person and I cannot think of anyone I admire or like better.

Ringo Starr, last to become a Beatle, came into the group not because I wanted him but because the boys did. To be completely honest, I was not at all keen to have him. I thought his drumming rather loud and his appearance unimpressive and I could not see why he was important to the Beatles. But again I trusted their instincts and I am grateful now. He has become an excellent Beatle and a devoted friend. He is warm and wry-witted, a good drummer, and I like him enormously. He is a very uncomplicated, very nice young man.

We rarely fall out because he, probably more than the others, is amenable to most suggestions. Yet there was one unpleasant incident at the start of the Paris trip early this year.

It was January and the Beatles were due to tackle a country in which – compared to, say, Scandinavia or Germany – they were an unknown quantity. Therefore I was anxious to make a good initial impact. This can be achieved, and the US trip proved it, at the arrival airport.

But fog descended over Liverpool and Ringo Starr could not leave for London to catch the connecting aircraft to Paris. The other Beatles and I and a score of journalists were in London when we heard the news. Naturally I was very disappointed that three Beatles instead of four would descend the steps at Le Bourget Airport in Paris. I telephoned Liverpool and asked Ringo to catch the train so that he could join up in Paris as soon as possible.

He refused, possibly because he believed that a Beatle shouldn't travel by train, and said he would catch the first available plane. I didn't want this because I didn't trust the weather and I said so.

I said: 'Ringo, I have never asked you to do anything especially for me before,' and he replied: 'Oh yes you have. You know bloody well you are always asking me to do things – to see the press, or travel for this or that. I'm not doing it and if you don't like it you can do the other thing.'

I was very angry and when, eventually, he arrived in Paris there was quite an atmosphere. But sulking has no place in a group like the Beatles and with just a couple of meaningful looks and a grin all was well. And, as with other difficulties, a frank talk helped. We get on extremely well, and later this year, George and Ringo came to live in the same block of flats as I do.

George too has his moods though I cannot recall any particular row. I don't enjoy arguments, nor do the Beatles, so we avoid anything too contentious. George is remarkably easy to be with. He, like the others, has expanded as a person, and though collectively – on first sight – they appear to behave alike, they have specific characteristics.

And George is the business Beatle. He is curious about money and wants to know how much is coming in and how and what best to do with it to make it work. He would like to invest. He is generous but shrewd. He enjoys spending but would always remain in credit. He likes cars, big and fast, but would be careful to secure a good trade-in price for his old one.

Strangers find him an easy conversationalist because he is a good listener and shows a genuine interest in the outside world. He wants to know and I find this an endearing trait in a young man who is so successful and so rich that if he never learned anything new he would not suffer any loss. And in addition to all these characteristics, he is, though not one of the prolific composers, very musicianly.

George takes enormous care with tuning before a show. He has a very fine ear for sound and for a delicate half-note and the others respect him for it. Onstage he is the one who twiddles the tuning instruments and you can almost see his ears twitching to detect a faint discord.

Virtually, if Paul has the glamour, John the command, Ringo the little man's quaintness, George with his slow, wide, crooked smile is the boy next door.

They are very fine extraordinary young men. I don't believe anything like them will happen again, and I believe that happen is the word since no one could have *created* anything in show business with such appeal and magnetism.

10

Nems

Nems Enterprises Ltd was formed in Liverpool in 1962, and in response to prolonged pressure for an admission on the point of money, I am prepared to admit that the company makes a pretty decent profit. I cannot, nor would I, discuss just how much, because in the first place I do not precisely know how much, and in the second place I detest financial arrogance.

I have witnessed the money-boaster, I have been saddened to read of his subsequent downfall and frightened much earlier than that by the signs of disaster. They are unmistakable and familiar and they alarm me. What I can say is that the money coming in is sufficient to ensure that everyone within the organisation is amply rewarded for the work they do. The Beatles are great stars and they receive the sort of money great stars are accustomed to receiving. Likewise Gerry, and all my artistes and staffs – ability is well regarded and well paid.

Nems was formed to handle the affairs of my artistes,

as an offshoot of the family business, and I retained the old initials of North End Music Stores chiefly because I didn't want to follow the showbiz pattern and call it the Brian Epstein Organisation or anything of that highly personalised sort.

At first, after I had signed the Beatles, I operated them as a private business and all of it I handled alone. I simply collected cash at the end of a week and I was grateful if it reached £100. On a very special week it might reach £180 and this made me very excited because it could mean that I made a small profit.

But as 1962 progressed, and Gerry and the Pacemakers joined me, I decided to form a limited company to cope with tax matters, to ease banking arrangements and generally put the growing band of artistes on a proper footing. My brother Clive joined me as a director and I registered Nems Enterprises Ltd in June that year.

I was, however, the entire working staff, for Clive was very busy with the family businesses. Natural growth and a little of Parkinson's Law demanded that I take on staff, and by the end of June, the new company had its first employee – Beryl Adams, a secretary who had worked with me before. We had offices on the first floor of the Whitechapel store in Liverpool which we retained even up to the middle of last year and which, on the local scene, became better known than the Liver Buildings, which dominate Liverpool's waterfront.

Whitechapel was a street where, on a lucky day, you might spot a Beatle or see Gerry buying a packet of cigarettes. Whitechapel became more beleaguered than an ancient fortress. And, eventually, so did I.

Pressures mounted and the staff increased. I took on a personal assistant, an ex-medical student, to deal with small matters, and I concentrated – as I still do now – on the promotion and welfare of the artistes.

A telephonist followed, then a typist. Suddenly our offices were too small and our business too big and in the summer of 1963 we moved to Moorfields, a charming little street near Exchange Station in Liverpool, and there we took a suite a few yards away from the Wizard's Den, the most famous magic shop in the North of England, where you can buy anything from a horror mask to a joke spider or maybe, like most of Liverpool, you don't buy anything. You just stand there and stare and remember when you were young and magic was a wonderful thing.

Into our offices in Liverpool we brought new furnishings, new people and a seething sense of urgency. A brand-new switchboard was installed with two telephonists. We took on office boys, a general manager, an accountant, a press officer, a fan-club staff who had to be set up in London. Also I needed a personal secretary, and thus we outgrew our new offices within six months.

But alas, and I regret this very profoundly, we also outgrew our beloved, lovely Liverpool.

The world over, there is, ultimately, only one place for a major enterprise and that place is the capital. It is sad and inconvenient but it is inescapable that in England the centre of show business is London. This I discovered and, with immense reluctance, I decided in the autumn of last year that I could resist London no longer. I instructed agents to look for offices and I warned my staff that the upheaval and the separation from their native city and its sounds were inevitable.

We chose our new offices in London next door to the London Palladium in Argyll Street, W1. Our neighbours, we argued, should be the biggest names in show business, for if we were to be forced to leave Liverpool, we might as well do it in style.

Much has been written in the newspapers about Nems deserting the city which had 'made' them and so on ... but the fact was that we had no choice. The move freed me from spending half my life either in the air or on a train shuttling between Liverpool and the capital; also it enabled me to bring all the staff together and to employ the sort of top-level executives who can only be found in London – a booking manager, a director of presentation and personal assistants.

Much earlier than this, the Beatles, Gerry and the Pacemakers, and Billy J. Kramer had all become limited companies; and by the end of 1963, so varied were the sources of income, and so substantial the amounts, that one of London's leading firms of chartered accountants found it necessary to regard Nems artistes as a major industry.

Our money comes in from all sides – from personal appearances, from discs, from television, radio and film work, from merchandising – the sale of Beatle wigs, talcum powder, chewing gum, guitars. Almost, literally, every product under the sun.

Merchandising can be profitable but figures of millions

of pounds in royalties from America are undistilled nonsense; I cannot myself estimate how much we will make because the year is not over and new products bear the name 'Beatle'. One of the features of merchandise is, by the way, its comparatively short life. A product will make an immediate novelty appeal but interest flags quite quickly.

All of us learned a solemn lesson when the Davy Crockett vogue died overnight, leaving frenzied wholesalers gazing in despair at hundreds of thousands of unsold coonskin hats.

To handle the sheet-music and publishing side of the business, John, Paul and I had linked with Dick James, an honourable and well-regarded publisher who had been a well-known band singer – he is the man singing the title song of television's *Robin Hood*.

When I met him he had a small publishing office but huge integrity. Now his power in publishing matches his character and I believe both are unequalled in London.

To handle songs written by John and Paul, the two composer-Beatles formed Northern Songs Ltd, with Dick. I also have a share in this company, though my major publishing interests are in Jaep Music Co. which is part owned by Dick and part by myself – Ja for the first part of Dick's surname, Ep for the first part of mine. This company handles material recorded by artistes of mine excepting the Beatles and Gerry and the Pacemakers.

Gerry has his own company, again with Dick, called Pacermusic, and this, like the others, is doing very nicely. We have been fortunate to have Dick with us, as one of the features of Nems is that we are surrounded by people who know their business and behave themselves.

As newcomers to show business, I and my early staff decided to associate only with the most honest of established experts. We were vulnerable enough to sharp practitioners without making friends with rogues, and as a result of our care in the beginning, we have created a team which is incorruptible, powerful and which has a sense of direction and purpose.

One of the chief factors in this business – as in all others – is timing and only after prolonged discussion between George Martin and myself, and after consultation with the artistes, is a song chosen and a disc released. I believe I know a hit when I hear one, but George Martin knows the record industry infinitely better than I ever could; and because George has been at it for some time, he has an innate sense of the public mood.

Thus we both pool our views, our flair and our experience before putting discs before the buyers and, up to now, our joint endeavours have been pretty successful. For in twenty months, Nems artistes have placed sixteen numbers at the top of the British Record Charts, in addition to countless list-toppers the world over.

This hasn't happened by accident and it can only be sustained by taking the greatest care, for though success breeds success we could easily topple if we tried to flood the market with shoddy goods. The public is no fool.

Though our artistes produce the records, though we – Dick James, the publisher, George Martin and myself – are the men immediately behind the discs, we are the tip of the iceberg. Beneath the surface is the huge imponderable unreliable mass of public taste, the song-pluggers and the disc jockeys, the television and radio men, the shifts in spending power – all the factors which can mean the difference, say, between Gerry making number one and a sale of 500,000 discs, or number five and half these sales.

The song-pluggers are fascinating men, very old hands at the game and everybody's friends. They have to place a song on this television show or that radio programme. They are diligent and full of enthusiasm and I don't know where we should all be without them.

The disc jockeys are an entirely different breed, for if the pluggers are the original faceless men, the DJs live almost entirely on personality and self. They are, in general, very vain men and considerably less powerful than they believe but I like most of them very much because they are happy extroverts and, usually, very amusing companions.

I think one of my favourites is Alan Freeman because he is fascinated by the charts. So also is Jimmy Savile who will often say the first thing that comes into his head, making wild, unjustifiable predictions with great, infectious gusto.

Brian Matthew, with whom I am involved in a non-pop theatrical venture in Bromley, Kent, is one of the more serious disc jockeys. He is with-it and accurate and, though it doesn't always show, a stern, cynical man.

He knows there is a lot of gloss and nonsense in the industry and offstage he makes no secret of his regard for what might be termed the 'higher' things of life. Brian is a great lover of discipline and he once reported one of my groups for fooling around on *Thank Your Lucky Stars*, which earned him my additional respect even if I didn't show it at the time.

David Jacobs is very shrewd, full of visual charm, poise and television-warmth. He is an immaculate DJ so far as musical taste is concerned and a very nice man. He is also the best-looking disc jockey and in the circumstances remarkably modest about it.

If I believe that the control on public taste of the DJ is limited, I take an entirely different view of the press, whose strength and influence only a fool would underestimate. They have power and they wield it exactly when, how and where they please and I cannot see any objection to this.

However, I must say that contrary to some claims, they had nothing to do with making the Beatles. I was amazed that they were so late on the scene and I was profoundly glad that I did not have to rely on newspapers to get the Beatles and Gerry away. For if I had, I would have lost at least a year and that would possibly have been too late.

The Beatles had taken 'Please Please Me' to the top of the charts and played to wild packed houses in every British city before any journalist beyond disc reviewers took an interest in this extraordinary new group and the city which had launched them.

The 'Mersey Sound', so called, had been noising loudly for more than eighteen months before an echo landed in any national newspaper office, but to give the press its due – and I always do – once they had discovered what was happening to popular music, they responded and reported with splendid vigour.

In the early days in Liverpool, two Rabelaisian members of the roaring, swinging press club there offered to form a promotion organisation called 'Publicity Ink', to operate on my behalf for a fee of £100 – without, of course, the knowledge of their newspaper employers – stunts, gimmicks, rows, scenes. Anything to get the names of my artistes in the papers.

The plan was conceived after much Draught Bass and whisky and it was lightly, though purposefully, pursued by these two reporters, but I had nothing to do with it and I'm glad now for it enables me to say that I never pulled one stunt to publicise any of my artistes.

It would have been easy, for instance, to hire a girl or two to leap onstage to mob Paul, or claim that each had received a proposal of marriage from Ringo or something of that sort. It had been done before and it will be done again but if you can get any substance from show business by those methods I should be very surprised.

I am very fond of journalists. I believe they are wonderful classless people with a great sense of democracy and an enviable zest for life. They are also very interesting to be with because they know something about everything and they know the news behind the news. Individually I find them splendid, though collectively they do not always behave terribly well, nor ask the most intelligent questions.

Sometimes I will manipulate the press without the slightest sense of guilt, for I know they would manipulate me if I allowed them. I employ, when I can, the envy of one paper for another's story; it is a great game and I believe we all enjoy it. I never bear malice and I trust journalists not to.

I believe we are all in this together, public, artistes, management, press, the entire entertainment industry, and I believe we should all, like Arnold Bennett's *Card*, be identified with the 'great cause of cheering us all up'.

11

Strain

I don't know whether it was William Shakespeare or Ringo Starr who said: 'When this business stops being fun, I'm giving it up,' but whoever it was I know what he meant and there was a time early this year when I almost gave it up.

The whole business became too much for me – the travelling and the telephone, the talk and the deals, the relentless social duties, the rootlessness of my life and the sheer hard slog of staying on top. For some months the strain had been building up, and I felt my life was an awful mess. Then suddenly, I realised that the power was entirely in my hands – I didn't have to go on any more. I could dispose of my interest in my artistes and live entirely as I pleased for the rest of my life, very comfortably off.

One night I went out with a columnist – he now works on my executive staff – and we had dinner at the Rembrandt Club in Liverpool. He was interviewing me for an article to be published on 14 January, to coincide with the Beatles' departure for their Paris season. We had talked on the usual subjects – the unprecedented success of the Beatles, its causes and effects, the future and so on. I said it was difficult to know about the future and the journalist said casually, in the way pressmen do: 'D'you think you'll ever sell the Beatles?'

I didn't reply for a moment and I looked away. He allowed the pause to continue, assuming, rightly, that the silence would embarrass me. I reached for a stick of celery and tapped it on my plate. 'It's a large question,' I said. 'I don't think I would.'

'Look at me in the eyes,' said the journalist, 'and say: I will never sell the Beatles.'

Again I looked away and I gave him no reply. I felt dreadful. I wouldn't have believed, six months earlier, that there would come a moment when I could entertain the slightest doubt about my future with the Beatles, or, for that matter, with any of my artistes.

But the truth was that I was, that very week, to decide whether or not I was staying in business as sole director of all the wonderful young people who had so changed my life. I had been made one hard, genuine cash-in-hand offer only that day of £150,000 for a share in the Beatles and three days later, in a London restaurant, I dined with the man who made the offer.

The offer was for a 50 per cent interest in all my artistes and management companies, to give me my capital gain of £150,000 and to allow me final say on the type of work the Beatles did and relieve the strain, but my power as a result would remain limited. Though I did not find it very attractive it would have been the end of much worry and strain.

I told my powerful companion: 'I need time. You know my views so far but there is one thing I must do. I must tell the Beatles.'

I formed a complete plan in my mind. I would sell the Beatles and all of my artistes except one whom I would still retain under sole direction. Of the other artistes I would become personal manager, and the agency with whom I would do the deal would take over all the headaches and a great deal of the income.

But first I had to see the Beatles. I met them in my flat and I said to them: 'How would you feel if —— took you over?' and George, without looking up, muttered: 'You're joking.'

'I've never been more serious in my life,' I said, and Ringo said: 'Tell us again.' I repeated: 'How would you feel? It's a very good agency.' Said John, the literary Beatle: 'Get stuffed.' Paul said something similar, though less polite, and I said: 'You don't seem very enthusiastic.'

They all looked at me as if I were mad. I said: 'You must know this. I'm not sure I can do everything I should for you. The organisation is getting very big and the pressure's a bit much. You might well be better off elsewhere.'

The Beatles were speechless. They had never imagined a split in our relationship and I argued as persuasively as I could that it could be in their own interests, though the longer I spoke the less I was convincing myself. At length, I stopped and said: 'Well?' Paul said: 'Sell us and we'll pack up completely. We'll throw the whole lot up tomorrow.'

This was all I needed and I was overwhelmed by their attitude. Their loyalty was tremendous and I feel I can never really repay it. Until then I don't feel I had ever realised its depth nor had I known how proud they were of me as their leader. I returned to the financier and I said: 'Thank you for your offer but I cannot accept it. I don't think all the money in the world would be enough.' He was very disappointed, and, I suspect, annoyed, but God gave us tongues to conceal our thoughts and he said, courteously enough: 'OK, Brian. Fair enough. It would have been a good deal, though.'

And this was the point. The Beatles are not a deal. They are unique human beings and I believe that even if the whole thing peters out I will always be with the Beatles. I would like to look after them in some way throughout their lives, not because I want a percentage but because they are my friends. Since those January doubts, I have not wavered in my determination to retain sole direction, for I could never be sure that anyone else would care for the artistes in the way they deserve. I believe, as modestly as I can, that they all need me.

The strain, however, continues and increases and thrives like a malignant disease. I know that thousands of executives in the provinces and, to a greater extent, in London have massive worries, work stupidly long hours, deprive themselves of exercise and leisure, but I do not know of anyone who works harder than I do. This is not boastful, for I am not particularly proud of it, nor is it very clever. But it's true.

The telephone in my office – I have two: one a direct

line, the other through a switchboard – does not stop for one second of any day. Mostly there are two calls on simultaneously, and an inter-office Dictaphone hammering the brain into a half-coma. It is one thing to have a good staff – and I have – but it is quite another to be able to delegate. I have never been good at this, and though I employ the sort of people who can make wise and honourable decisions, I am loath to give them the power to do so, for by making my own mind up I remain sure that there is an overall design.

I believe in democracy but I also like to see one man clearly in charge, answerable to himself for his own mistakes. There are penalties. The chief of them is loneliness, for ultimately I must bear the strain alone, not only in the office or the theatre, but at home in the small hours. When a disc goes badly or a business venture fails, I am the one who suffers most, for I hold myself responsible. It isn't the money that worries me; it's the failure. Though I didn't seek it, fame has overtaken me and this is not always very pleasant; partly because of my youth, partly because of my background and provincial origins, my sudden entry into show business with the greatest stars in the world, I am sought now by pressmen, by fans, by all manner of people as I never wished to be.

Eighteen months ago when the first national newspaperman came to interview me, I was withdrawn, awkward, edgy and not at all anxious to talk about myself. For about three minutes I refused to say in which part of Liverpool I lived, not because I was ashamed but because I could not see its relevance. Now, from habit,

I have become almost a professional interviewee and my chief anxiety is guarding against glibness. Since that first interview I have, I believe, been grossly over-exposed – a danger of which everyone around the Beatles is acutely aware – not only in print but in vision. *Panorama* 'did' me earlier this year, and I have appeared on practically every independent channel, constantly probed and scratched in an endeavour to discover the success of my artistes. (The answer to this is very simple – they are talented people.)

Mr Kenneth Harris, who is normally more at home with Premiers and Archbishops, did one of those searching face-to-face articles on me for the *Observer*, and twice I submitted myself to searching interviews on BBC Radio. Finally by midsummer 1964 the situation became so serious that I had to turn down an offer of a forty-minute profile on BBC2, and a writer on a magazine called *The New Elizabethan* phoned me to say, 'Would you mind if we didn't do that article on you ... we feel you've been rather well done already.'

He can say that again.

Of course, it is all very flattering. It was nice to be asked to telecast the 'Week's Good Cause'. I liked being named as one of the Ten Best Dressed men. Everyone likes to matter, but it can go too far. One begins to feel like a goldfish, swimming round and round simply to help other people relax. There are, also, a few fan problems which became more acute when George and Ringo came to live in the same block of flats and there is now not a daylight hour when the hall doorway isn't darkened by a knot of autograph hunters, some hardly out of their prams.

At first when I was asked for autographs it was quite pleasurable – nice to be noticed and recognised – but it has since become not only a chore but perilous.

One night after a 'Mod' Ball at Wembley Pool, on which several of my artistes had been appearing, a screaming pack of fifty girls encircled me as I was leaving the building. They tore at my coat and pinned my arms by my sides and I was about to be pulled to the ground when from the shadows leapt Neil Aspinall, the agile Beatles' road manager, who dived through them and had me clear in four or five seconds.

Never have I been so thankful to see anyone nor so grateful of Neil's experience in saving the Beatles from death day by day.

Older fans are not so violent but they are not nearly as pleasant. On my way to Torquay one night to start work on this book, I stopped off for a last-minute drink at a hotel in Windsor. It was just on closing time and my assistant and I ordered two stiff brandies. At the other end of the bar were five men in evening dress all of whom were staring at me. One of them swayed over and said: 'My friend says you're the Beatles' boss. I've got a pound says you're not. What about it?' I said 'I am' and he said, pushing the pound in my face: 'This says you're not.' I replied, trying to get on with my drink: 'All I can tell you is that I am and would you mind letting me have a quiet drink?'

'What's your name then?' said the man, supporting himself on the bar.

'Brian Epstein,' said my assistant, and the other four men then came over. They demanded that I produced my driving licence and finally agreed that I was who I claimed to be.

The men then insisted that we have a drink, that their wives meet us, that we discussed the Beatles and that we sign autographs not only for them but for their children.

As Ringo says 'this is the penalty of being the Beatles' manager' and he should know, for the prohibitions and inhibitions of a Beatle's life are unimaginably severe.

A Beatle must not marry. It is all very well if one is married before one is a fully grown Beatle but a fully grown Beatle must stay single. He cannot pop into the local cinema or snatch a quick pint in the local, for if he does, not only will he spend the entire time signing autographs, he may also be insulted ... 'Why are you so big-headed? What's so special about you? Your hair's too long ... your music's lousy ...'

A Beatle must not go abroad for a holiday with his girlfriend for, if he does, Mr John Gordon of the *Sunday Express* will thunder about moral example, not mentioning, of course, that practically every teenager in the land holidays with a member of the opposite sex.

This year, for example, the Beatles' holiday was to be gloriously private. It was planned weeks ahead and it was arranged like this. We sidestepped our regular travel agents – excellent though they are – because they are too well known. Instead we hired another company and told them we wanted a foolproof secret route plotting for four young men and three girlfriends and a wife. The men, we explained, would travel in pairs, the girls, one pair, two singles. We wanted two destinations, at which two sets of couples would link up.

None of the arrangements were to be made by phone and code names were created for the eight. Mr McCartney was Mr Manning; Mr Starr was Mr Stone. Their companions were to be Miss Ashcroft and Miss Cockcroft. Mr Lennon was Mr Leslie, and his wife, Mrs Leslie. Mr Harrison was Mr Hargreaves and his girlfriend became Miss Bond. Manning and Stone, Ashcroft and Cockcroft were to holiday in the Virgin Islands; the Leslies, Hargreaves and Bond would go to Tahiti.

These were the routes: Manning, Stone to fly in disguise by charter plane from Luton to Paris, thence, after a tarmac transfer, by Air France Caravelle to Lisbon. The girls to fly BEA London to Lisbon. Link with boys at Lisbon for through flight to Puerto Rico. There to split again and link later with yacht for month's cruise.

The Leslies and Hargreaves charter flight, Luton to Amsterdam, Miss Bond BEA to Amsterdam, link with other three thence to Vancouver en route finally for Honolulu and Tahiti for yacht.

At 8 a.m., on Saturday, 2 May, security solid, secrecy

absolute and stomachs fluttering nervously, eight figures huddled in doorways around London. Every Beatle home and those of their girlfriends are watched constantly by press and fans, and to guard against early discovery, the eight had stayed the previous night in the homes of other people.

Small hired chauffeured cars made their rendezvous in the doorways. Travel agents sworn to silence, close friends and employees travelled with them to the pick-up point. With Paul and Ringo travelled my personal assistant Derek Taylor, travelling as Tatlock. With Patti Boyd (alias Bond) went Neil Aspinall, travelling as Ashenden.

Paul in blue-tinted sunglasses, sinister slim moustache, hair slicked back under a huge hat was unrecognisable. Likewise Ringo, in black hat, with drooping ginger moustache and hornrims. Together they looked like spies in an old Paul Henreid film. Beatles never.

The first stages of all journeys passed without recognition. Both quarters reached their major staging point. But somehow, and no one will ever know, when George and John reached Vancouver there were three hundred fans to meet them. And Puerto Rico went wild when the two 'spies' flew in.

The secret was out and weeks of minute arrangement were squandered. The result was autograph hunters, imprisonment in a hotel for two days for John and George, *Daily Express* men in a speedboat seeking – and, *Express*-fashion, finding – Paul and Ringo.

Is this a holiday?

Well, in the end it was, and a good one, but it is an illustration of the other side of being a Beatle.

And the final seal was set on this venture when, after the boys returned, a Fleet Street editor said to me: 'You managed to leak the holiday plans very nicely, Brian ...'

Sometimes, I feel, you cannot win.

12

Tomorrow

Whatever happens tomorrow, one thing is certain: it must not be allowed to look after itself. For tomorrow is the cardinal problem and it must be tightly under my control.

Yesterday was a wonderful day. It was warm and dry and the sun shone and the Beatles were brilliant and the others too. Today is nice too. There's still no change in the weather, except for the faintest breeze which suggests we must be on guard. Probably it might be as well to carry our raincoats tomorrow. Then it won't rain.

It's a great privilege being the weatherman, keeping the Beatles and Billy J. and Cilla dry and comfortable. I enjoy it far too much to relax, but of course, I cannot see too far into the future so it's no use asking me how long it can go on. 'How long will the Beatles last?' you ask. And some of you say, 'It's only a craze really.'

Well, I don't know how long the Beatles will last and neither do they. Nobody does but the barometer looks very promising. They are the biggest attraction the entertainment industry has ever known, or will know, and this sort of bigness doesn't dissolve overnight or even in a year. I believe that really the future is entirely up to the Beatles and to me. If we are very careful we may keep on making show-business history, by bridging not only the gulf between the ages of fans – they did that a year ago – but by stepping over their own age problems.

George Harrison wrote in his *Daily Express* column months ago: 'We obviously can't go around as Beatles when we're in our forties,' and to an extent this is true. But so fast have they developed and expanded up to now, that they may, changing imperceptibly, month by month and stage by stage, become an extraordinary force in other branches of entertainment.

I see tremendous possibilities in films and this may well be the way I shall guide them. Clearly they cannot be expected to tour the country on one-night stands, living out of suitcases year after year, issuing a disc every three months. But the Beatles themselves delight in personal appearances – audience response is their only stimulant drug – and any change from present policy must be gently and easily effected.

How do I handle them and the other artistes? Well, I remember primarily that I am their manager and not their keeper. Nor am I a parent with a duty to teach them manners, how to speak or hold their forks. I am not a schoolmaster to make them read or cultivate themselves. I am most certainly not their judge on morals or behaviour.

I am, simply, their guide and I am not myself absolutely certain how it has all happened. I try to ease them into doing a song in this order or that order in a show, and, similarly, merely hint that this style of suit is right for that singer. Imperfect as we all are, example is also useful, and I believe that as I have learned from the Beatles so they have picked up some good habits from me. From Gerry I have been taught something of the benefit of robust earthiness. From me he may have learned a little repose.

From Cilla Black, a beautiful lady, all of us have drawn something.

She is what she is – an untutored girl from a large, happy, working-class family in a lowly part of Liverpool. She may not curtsy by instinct, but she is warm and natural and frank and this may be far more important than protocol.

Yet one night when I took a famous man to see her, he said later: 'You will, of course, be teaching that young lady how to behave with a star like me. After all I am a household name and she didn't exactly acknowledge this.'

Said I: 'I thought she was rather nice,' and though he may not have known it, Cilla thought *he* was a decent sort of chap. The difference between them was that she made no remarks behind his back. I shall never attempt to dragoon my artistes into unnatural postures, for the very reason I engage performers is that I see in them a quality of stardom which, if warped or altered, would be lost.

The Beatles remain an extension of their early selves. They are older and wiser and they have absorbed some sophistication, but it is still their naturalness which wins them the admiration of people like Lord Montgomery – a straight man himself – and involves the Prime Minister and the Leader of the Opposition in voluble, rival claims to the ownership of the Beatles.

I have never actually made a star. The material is woven when I buy it over a sixpenny stamp on a contract. But I am a demon for balancing the careers of my artistes so that when, for instance, Billy J. Kramer left for his first major US trip, his first American disc release was heading for number one in the US charts.

Billy provides another example of balancing and planning. This summer he and his group, fresh from the number-one hold on the British charts with 'Little Children', entered what seemed to be a doldrum period. Billy said: 'We're not getting enough work,' though in fact they were starring in one theatre or another or on TV more often than he had noticed. I was faced with either (A) filling in odd nights with unsatisfactory dates or (B) building his morale with talk of first-class bookings already established for the near future. I explained the alternatives. He insisted: 'I'd like to be working non-stop, Brian.'

'Right,' I said. 'You can do ballrooms if you want for £400 a night. Is this what you want?' He had to agree that it was not, for at that stage in his career ballrooms were over. They were part of his development but they were in the past. He saw the reasoning and he said: 'OK, I'll just be patient,' and patient he was and he was a huge success in America three weeks later.

I'm convinced that many a manager or agent, faced with an impatient artiste and also a chance of a few hundred in commission, would have put the artiste out to the ballrooms the following week. Therein lies the road to nothing, for I believe that there are only two worthwhile routes in show business – up or out.

The most satisfying feature of my life in show business is that I enjoy it. I like artistes enormously – all artistes. I like meeting them, I like being amongst them, I enjoy their conversation, and I derive tremendous satisfaction from developing new artistes.

I think the best part of the business is guiding and watching the progress of newcomers, because after all the pop business is very much a business for new people. Without them popular music would die, and this, probably, is the reason why, although I am far too busy to be handling more artistes than I already have, I sign up fresh talent from time to time.

Certainly the Beatles themselves are a full-time job, but now that they are top of the world their challenge to me has diminished and I work better with a challenge than with a *fait accompli*. I find the pop scene fascinating and probably the most intriguing feature is the imponderable 'What makes a hit?'

This is unanswerable but one does develop an instinct, and I am a great believer in tunes. Although not all records get to the top of the hit parade because they are great tunes, generally speaking melody sells. Sir Thomas Beecham once said this at the Liverpool Philharmonic Hall when I was there as a boy. He said: 'I'm often asked why operas survive generation after generation – *La Bohème* and things like that. And I always reply: "They survive because they consist of bloody good tunes."'

Naturally songs without good tunes also get to the top of the hit parade. 'Please Please Me' was not a great tune but it was an exciting new sound, as was the Animals' 'House of the Rising Sun'.

Tunes can go wrong because a great deal happens to a tune in a recording studio, particularly nowadays when so many electronic devices and dodges are available. But basically if you can get a good melody that is going to suit the artiste and, equally important, if the artiste is going to like it, you are almost home and dry with a hit.

I have known good tunes to be spoiled by rotten recordings, either because the people who are singing them have not been able to cope with the song or haven't liked it.

The outstanding example of this in my experience is 'How Do You Do It?', which the Beatles rejected because they didn't like it although they knew it was a good tune, and which of course Gerry made a great success. There have been other examples recently – the Fourmost had a hit with 'A Little Lovin'' by Russell Alquist, who then brought up what I thought were three very good melodies for a follow-on disc.

The Fourmost recorded two of these numbers but I knew, and they knew, that they didn't like them. They didn't do a good job, and consequently the records weren't released, but later we found more numbers for the Fourmost which they did very well. There are no hard and fasts in the pop world.

I am often asked whether I think a lot of the stuff in the hit parade is rubbish, and I could not agree less. Very little rubbish makes any progress in the charts although occasionally – very occasionally – some frightful nonsense is bought but I think less now than ever.

Some problems I have still not solved, although the past three years have taught me how to tackle most of the snags which crop up from day to day when you are dealing with artistic people, with a fickle public and with people with far greater experience than I. One of the problems I still have to tackle is what to do about an artiste who I know to be good, who has material I know to be good, and yet who cannot produce a hit.

Such a man is Tommy Quickly who is extraordinarily popular with audiences, an amiable young man and a very good singer. He made a record which came from America called 'You Might As Well Forget Him'. It was extremely good and everybody in the business, including the Beatles and my other artistes, thought it was tremendous. We made a very good recording of it and the fans went wild over it at concerts. But it failed dismally. Not a thing happened to it.

One of the first lessons I learned in show business was that agents were not as bad as people had told me. Like everything else in life, when you get to know them they take shapes and forms as individuals – like restaurants and people you get to know very well – there are some good, some nice, some bad, some sharp, there are some who mean well and some who don't mean well at all.

I find, curiously enough, that the most difficult agents are those who have only been in the business a short time and I find this now after only having been in the business three years. Agents who suddenly have success can also be difficult, and I know that as my success was fairly immediate this could apply to me. I trust I am not too difficult.

I know one man who is becoming almost impossible. He is the manager of a well-known group and he has recently done very well with another group. He is quickly getting himself a very bad name because suddenly, because his groups are doing well, he is becoming difficult with managers and agents who previously in the early and lean days offered the groups work, and he is telling them, 'Oh no. Now they've done well we can't go ahead with such and such a contract.'

Now this is a thing I never did. By and large I went along with all the things I'd agreed to, and I didn't let pieces of paper stand in my way if I'd agreed to it verbally. I stood by contracts. With the exception that if I thought that a very unfair advantage was being taken I too could be difficult.

The Beatles themselves carried out all the dates in their £25, £50, £60 bracket even though by the time the dates arrived they were in a very much bigger fee bracket. Likewise Gerry and all my other groups. Many people forget that contracts are frequently arranged many months ahead and an artiste who in July can attract a fee of £1,000 a week may still have to fulfil a contract fixed in January at £100 a week.

The Beatles for instance played *The Ed Sullivan Show* in February – a contract fixed in the previous November when they were not important in America. They received about £1,000 a show – that would be about 10,000 dollars for the three shows – but the top rate which they could probably have asked for in February was about 7,000 dollars a show and possibly a little bit more. Not that it matters because the main thing is to fulfil contracts and exchange good will with good people.

I am constantly being confronted with people who have new talent to offer – either their own or their artistes'. I quite honestly have not the time to go into the talents of every individual, but I still believe that were a new Beatles to emerge it would be impossible for me to overlook them, as my Beatles were overlooked in 1962 by people who should have known better but didn't.

I enjoy the spirit of rivalry in show business. It is so strong that it provokes a great deal of healthy competitive mania and I find it most stimulating. The record charts have been criticised but I believe them to be very reasonable, very fair and extremely honest. The charts are one of my chief delights. The Beatles of course are not really in competition with anyone any more. I believe they, in their modest way, are enormously proud to have beaten the world and to have done it all with our own organisation rather than having to be tied up in any way with one of the big London groups. We take great pride in what has been termed the provincial breakthrough.

I think that as time goes on my relationship with older elements in show business mellows. At first they thought of me as a young upstart, and one who would inevitably fall. I think a lot of them hoped I would, but I didn't and now my acceptability is complete. Other people in the business still find me very remote, and all over the world this has been said of me – that I am aloof and stand apart and to a certain extent this is true. It is not studied – it is simply me.

This may seem curious in a necessarily extrovert world like Tin Pan Alley but the combination of me and pop music seems to work and consequently I don't mind people delving deep into me, searching for reasons and secrets, because there is nothing too bad there. Even if there were something to be ashamed of, if it were true and it were known and it were published I could not complain. I am extremely fond of the truth and I wish I could find it as often as I find the reverse in my day-by-day contacts with people.

It is fascinating in the pop context – in the competitive field of young people making their own music – to guide the development of my artistes. So many mistakes have been made by other managers, directors and agents that the lessons are plain and alarming and I trust I will not make too many. Most certainly the Beatles must be guided with great skill and it is doubtful at this stage that they will make many more personal appearance tours overseas.

Morale is vital. I do everything I can to sustain it at the highest level, and though I can often ill-afford time away from the desk and the telephone, I travel thousands – tens of thousands – of miles to be with my artistes at important times and at times not so important, whether it is the Palladium – as it has been for Cilla in her triumphant year, and for the Fourmost – or at the pub in Bolton where

I discovered Michael Haslam. I will be there because it really is what I exist for.

If I go to America with Billy, I cannot cry off when Gerry goes. If the Beatles make a film, then I must cast around for a film vehicle for the others. This is not to feed any envy; it is simply one's duty as a manager.

There are occasions, however, when my influence is limited. I can suggest this show or that song because they have a bearing on professional development. I could, though I haven't, object to a choice of clothing. But I am powerless in the private lives of my artistes beyond asking them to keep them separate from their working lives.

In 1963 Paul McCartney started to go out with a pretty young actress, Jane Asher. The press found out and there has been a daily rumour since of marriage – in London, Paris, New York or wherever else couples marry. Both Jane and Paul know that it is unwise for pop singers to marry and so they stay single. But if they were determined to wed, there is nothing I would wish to do to stop them.

Similarly with Ringo and George, both of whom have had their names linked with attractive girls. Though I believe the Beatles are a more solid unit without girls in the foreground, they have a right as citizens and human beings to go out with whom they please. They are not slaves, either to me or to their contracts, or, indeed to show business.

The time will come, of course, when they will marry and so, if I can get two days off, may I. And when this happens I must be sure that my own organisation is strong enough to endure the changes.

The Beatles may move more and more into films; most of the remaining artistes will endure and mature but I am anxious to build on the foundation of the beat groups and create other enterprises.

In Michael Haslam I have my first ballad singer; a 24-year-old tanner from Lancashire. He, I believe, is going to be very big. Later in 1964 I signed two non-Liverpool groups – the Ruskies and Cliff Bennett and the Rebel Rousers. In Sounds Incorporated I had already signed my first entertainers not from the North. The reason for a slight shift from beat is not because I see an end of heavy amplified guitar rhythm but because one must be able, literally, to call the tune. A 'hit', after all, is simply the song which is most popular at any given time. It need not be part of a trend – the Bachelors have proved this – it is far more likely to be the best disc available, whether 'Ramona' or 'Rock Around the Clock'.

I have known some failure in the midst of the winning streak. I attempted to bring Pops into the West End on Sunday night. All the top groups and soloists played week by week in elegant Prince of Wales Theatre on Piccadilly Circus. The quality was there but the fans weren't and I lost a good deal of money, none of which I regret because I learned a lesson and I was happy to have attempted something new.

My income permits me to spread into legitimate theatre, in which few make a fortune, and I have, as I said, invested in a new little theatre in Bromley, Kent, with Brian Matthew. Later I intend to buy a wonderful American musical for one of my own artistes. I should also like to direct or play in a straight drama without the slightest interest in profit, for I am not concerned with great wealth.

Though my terms with artistes are well known – friendship and 25 per cent all-in on top fees – I am, I fear, accused of greed. I am thought of as a hard businessman. In fact I am neither greedy nor hard but I am deeply concerned in preserving the status and upward climb of artistes. This is what they pay me 25 per cent for.

And if, through no manipulation of mine, the fees for top artistes are high – and, incidentally, I believe they are ridiculously high – then those are the fees I must charge. The fees were there when I was still selling furniture, and if Star X is worth £1,500 a week, I must charge more for the Beatles.

I could, I suppose, be hugely rich but I cannot see what good it would do me. I live well and spend largely and buy things I like, but I always did, and if I stopped earning tomorrow I could quite easily decimate my standard of living and still have a wonderful life. Though I adore eating and wining in, say, the Caprice in London, I am happier still in a small country restaurant.

However much I socialise with the great and famous, I would prefer a quiet afternoon with George Martin and Judy, making a bob or two at Lingfield Park races. And best of all and far beyond anything money can buy, I love to lean on my elbows at the back of the stalls and watch the curtain rise on John, Paul, George and Ringo, Gerry, Billy, Tommy, Michael – or the wonderful songbird daughter of a Liverpool docker and christened Priscilla

Maria Veronica White who will stun the world as Cilla Black. Tomorrow?

I think the sun will shine tomorrow.

Illustrations

The early days ... a sprinkling of memories.

The Beatles in the leather-jacketed Hamburg days, 1961.
Photo: Daily Express.

The engaging hit-paraders, Gerry and the Pacemakers.
Photo: Robert Freeman.

The signing of Billy J.

The Boys – with the Master. *Photos:* top, *Life Magazine*;
bottom, left, *Robert Freeman.*

Brian announces the name 'Beatles' at a Liverpool
concert. *Photo: Graham Spencer.*

Just for the camera. Brian and double bass. *Photo: Robert
Freeman.*

Early morning at Liverpool Docks. *Photo: Lewis Morley.*

The EMI recording studio in St John's Wood. *Photos:
Robert Freeman.*

Reflections Parisian. *Photo: Daily Express.*

Brian and car. *Photo: Robert Freeman.*

Relaxing with his parents. *Photo: Lewis Morley.*

Triumphant return. *Photo: Dezo Hoffman Ltd.*

Miami, February 1964. *Photos: Dezo Hoffman Ltd.*

Tycoonery. *Photos: Robert Freeman.*

Epstein and the artistes. *Photos:* top, right, *Dezo Hoffman Ltd.*; bottom, left, *Life Magazine*; others, *Robert Freeman.*

Brian in a mirror of his Knightsbridge flat. *Photo: Robert Freeman.*

It could be his home – but it is not. *Photo: Robert Freeman.*

Brian Epstein and the Beatles at their Royal Film Premiere. *Photo: Barratt's Photo Press.*

The presentation of the Carl-Alan Awards. *Photo: Associated Newspapers.*

The photos from *Life Magazine* are acknowledged to Terence Spencer-*Life Magazine* © 1964 Time Inc.

Acknowledgement is also due to the *Daily Mail* for their kind permission to reproduce the Flook cartoon.